SPIRITUAL

BEAUTY TREATMENTS

You Are
Beautiful!!!
Ecc. 3:11

Dixie Nash

DIXIE NASH

Spiritual Beauty Treatments

Your Transformation into Royalty

A Woman's Devotional

Dixie Nash

ISBN 13 TP: 978-0-7684-8426-7

ADVANCED GLOBAL PUBLISHING, INC.
P.O. Box 310, Shippensburg, PA 17257-0310

For Worldwide Distribution, Printed in the U.S.A.

1 2 3 4 5 6 7 8 9 10 11 12 13 14

Dedication

This book is dedicated to my daughters, Necia and Trisha. You are two of the most beautiful women of God that I know. You inspire and encourage me to be all that God desires me to be. I am truly honored to be your mother. I love you deeply.

Acknowledgments

This book was a family effort. My daughters, Necia and Trisha suggested physical beauty treatments to complement the spiritual beauty treatments. My son, Shea, helped me develop a format for the devotionals. My son in law, Phil, thought I should develop a website so that women can buy the beauty products that are recommended in the book. *www.spiritualbeautytreatments.com* is where you will find them for your convenience. My husband, Jim, has been my rock and helped steer the course during this new adventure. I am very grateful to my family for believing in me and encouraging me along the way to becoming an author. Thank you to Becky, Julia and Elsie for editing the manuscript. Thank you to Rebecca for enjoying the journey with me. I am very grateful to God for people who reflect His love of details. Finally, I want to thank Holy Spirit for the joy it is to work with Him. You have the best ideas Holy Spirit!

Contents

INTRODUCTION

THE PLAN UNFOLDS

Queen Esther went through a whole year of beauty treatments before she met her future husband, King Xerxes. Six months of oil of myrrh, and six months with perfumes and cosmetics (Esther 2:9,12). Wow, that is a lot of preparation! I woke up one morning thinking about Esther's beauty treatments and decided that I would ask the Holy Spirit for spiritual beauty treatments to send to my daughter, via email, who was a missionary in Nepal helping women who have come out of trafficking.

The first spiritual beauty treatment that came to my mind was the oil of joy. And then, the Lord unfolded a plan that would help women step into the royal position that Christ Jesus has created for them.

1 Peter 2:9 "But you are a chosen people,
a royal priesthood, a holy nation, a people belonging to God,
that you may declare the praises of him who called you out
of darkness into his wonderful light."

My family got excited when I shared with them the idea of spiritual beauty treatments. After much discussion, as to how to offer spiritual beauty treatments to share with others, it was decided that I explain the application process and then present the devotionals in a book. I pray that these spiritual beauty treatments will bring about the great beauty within and without that God has originally designed for you.

- Dixie

Beginning Your  Transformation

Beauty is not only about what your skin and your external appearance look like. Beauty is often revealed through the inner and outer atmosphere a person creates, the way you carry yourself through life, and knowing your value and worth. As you read this book, there are a couple of steps you need to take towards connecting, or reconnecting, with the One who created you to be beautiful and longs for a restoration of your beauty that comes with cultivating the inner atmosphere with the spirit of God.

First and foremost it is vital to have a personal relationship with the King of Kings, Jesus, as he has all the beauty in the world within himself to give to you. He is so excited to share his creative beauty with you! If you have not asked Jesus to be your savior, you can do so now by praying this prayer: "Father God, forgive my sins. Jesus, come into my heart. Make me the kind of person you want me to be. Thank you for saving me, Jesus. Amen"

If you just prayed that prayer you have just connected with the King of the Universe and you now have eternal life with Him. You also have received the inner beauty of the spirit of God. This inner beauty releases the creative power that shifts you from being an ordinary woman, to being a woman of influence. No longer a poor orphan, you will realize your value in the eyes of God and begin to step into the journey of discovering your worth.

"Now this is eternal life: that they may know you, the only true God, and Jesus Christ, whom you have sent".
John 17:3

You have completed the essential first step in applying these spiritual beauty treatments. Now for the second step, this is a reliance on the Holy Spirit as your teacher. Pray for the Holy Spirit to fill your heart and mind with His presence.

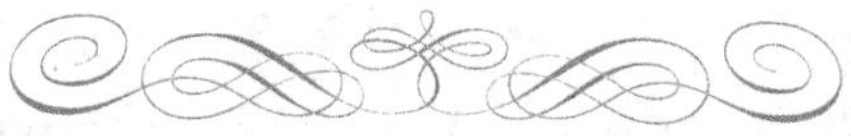

"But when he, the Spirit of truth, comes, he will guide you into all truth. He will not speak on his own; he will speak only what he hears, and he will tell you what is yet to come. He will bring glory to me by taking from what is mine and making it known to you. All that belongs to the Father is mine. That is why I said the Spirit will take from what is mine and make it known to you." John 16:13–15

We must listen to the Holy Spirit to be able to apply the spiritual beauty treatments. The Holy Spirit may speak to you through scripture that seems to jump off the page at you, which can be called a spiritual highlighting. He may speak to you in a picture in your mind's eye. As it says in Ephesians 1:18, *"I pray also that the eyes of your heart may be enlightened in order that you may know the hope to which he has called you, the riches of his glorious inheritance in the saints..."*

Or He may speak to you in an inaudible or audible voice. Whatever He instructs, it will always line up with scripture and God's character and nature. This is the plumb line that we follow when we receive instructions from the Holy Spirit.

Spiritual Applications

As you read, you may wonder how you are to apply the spiritual beauty treatments. Here is a guide to understanding.

Oil: If the beauty treatment is oil, it is to be smeared on or rubbed in. This is the meaning of being anointed.[1]Ask the Holy Spirit to apply the oil where needed upon your soul or body. Essential oils penetrate deeply into your cells. When Queen Esther applied the oil of myrrh, the essence of the oil would have gone deep into her body melding with her cells.[2]She would have given off the aroma of the myrrh. It would have become a part of who she was.

1 Strong, James, S.T.D., LL.D., Strongs Hebrew and Greek Dictionaries, e-Sword, Dictionary "Chrio", G5548

2 Studies of essential oils, such as myrrh, show that they absorb into the body quickly. Essential Oils Desk Reference, (Essential Science Publishing, 2006) 8.

Myrrh oil has many health benefits, which you can research on your own. But for our purposes of spiritual beauty treatments; just know that when you ask the Holy Spirit to apply spiritual oil to your life, it will penetrate deeply into your being becoming a part of you and affecting all that you do.

Spirit: When applying a beauty treatment of Spirit, such as "a quiet and gentle spirit" (1 Peter 3:4), we know that every spirit that Jesus wants us to apply is HOLY. Holiness is the essence of God. To be holy means to be morally pure, blameless and sacred.[3] In the Bible the Holy Spirit is depicted in symbolism as wine. Ephesians 5:18 reads: *"Do not get drunk on wine, which leads to debauchery. Instead, be filled with the Spirit."* Even in the world people will refer to alcohol as "spirits". So when applying a beauty treatment of spirit ask the Holy Spirit to fill you so you can spiritually drink in the particular beauty aspect that is brought up in the devotions. When we drink something it affects our well-being and becomes a part of our system.

Bathe: Sometimes you will be asked to apply a beauty treatment by bathing. This means to soak

---

3 Strong, James, S.T.D., LL.D., Strongs Hebrew and Greek Dictionaries, e-Sword, Dictionary "Hagios", G40.

or meditate. Again, ask the Holy Spirit to have the beauty treatment go deep into your soul and body. This can be for cleansing beauty treatments as well as for restorative purposes.

Food: Queen Esther also ate special foods as part of her beauty treatments (Esther 2:9). Some of these spiritual beauty treatments you may want to partake of as spiritual food where you taste and see that it is good. You chew on the word for a while (You would be getting all of the nutrients in this spiritual food that you can). Then you may need to digest the spiritual food (take time) and let it process. You may even need to process it by talking to others about this beauty treatment. Finally, it enters your system and brings you life, energy and power.

Prophetic Act or Sign: Sometimes there will be a suggestion to do something as a prophetic act or sign. This means that the act you will be performing is a sign or symbol of the spiritual truth you believe to be true.

Solo Devotional or Group Bible Study

This book can be used as a personal devotional book or, as a group Bible study. Either way can be full of fun and a delightful way to delve into the nature of God's love and rise higher into your own self-worth.

There are twelve themes for the spiritual beauty treatments with seven applications for each theme. There will be physical beauty treatment applications that you can apply, along with a scripture and a short devotional. Take as much time as you need to reap the benefits of each devotion. There are scripture references after each devotion so you can go deeper in your knowledge and understanding of your beautiful relationship with God.

Remember there is a website where you can purchase some of the beauty products that are suggested in the devotions to apply physically, *www.spiritualbeautytreatments.com*.

You will have to do your own research on the physical beauty products. Please use your own discretion as to what you use on your body. Consult with your doctor first if you have any allergies to specific physical products.

I encourage you to journal your thoughts and discoveries so you can better see the transformation into your royal beauty. You may want to discuss with a friend or Bible study group, what you discover with each devotion. If appropriate, it would be fun to do some of the physical beauty treatments as a group. If this book is being used in a Bible study setting, you might want to choose two or three themes and then read one or two devotions a week. Discuss how to go about putting the beauty treatments into action. Then look up the scriptures in the "going deeper" section. If a devotion brings up a prayer need, be sure and pray for one another. The following week, start the session with what was learned while applying the spiritual and physical beauty treatments of the previous week before looking at the next devotion. These beauty treatments will refresh, restore and renew you. May the blessing of the Holy Spirit be upon us as we come to feel as beautiful as we truly are in the eyes of our Lord Jesus Christ.

Joy

Delicious Joy

"But the fruit of the Spirit is... joy..." (Galatians 5:22, NIV)

Joy is a fruit of the Holy Spirit. Scripture tells us to taste and see that the Lord is good (Psalm 34:8). We find this true because his fruit of joy is delicious! Fruit starts out in seed form, so ask Holy Spirit to plant joy in your heart. Then you and He nurture it so that it will grow into full fruition. You do this by noticing when you have joy and then rejoice even more with praise to God. If you already have the full fruit of joy in your life, share it with others. When joy has matured, it is like a full-bodied wine spreading its effervescing quality into the atmosphere around you. Joy does not depend on circumstances. Joy comes from knowing God's love and is a gift.

This week, take note of joy coming out of you and develop it by giving thanks to God for this delectable fruit. Place yourself in environments of joy to catch the flavor of life in the Holy Spirit! Also eat fruit that brings you joy as a reminder of God's fruit of joy.

Going Deeper: Read the following scriptures: Psalm 86:4, Mark 4:26-29, Galatians 5:22. What new insight is Holy Spirit giving you, or what truth is going deeper into your soul?

Prayer Time: Ask the Lord to increase joy in your life.

ANOINTED WITH JOY

"...God, your God has set you above your companions by anointing you with the oil of joy."

(Hebrews 1:9, NIV)

This scripture passage is referring to Jesus. He was/ is the happiest man on earth. He lives inside you by His Holy Spirit and wants you to experience this joy. The Greek word for this kind of joy is agalliasis,[1] which means "exuberant joy." This kind of joy requires some kind of action to express this much joy - actions such as jumping up in the air, singing, shouting or dancing. Ask Holy Spirit to rub in and anoint you spiritually with this oil of joy so that it will permeate your entire being.

---

1 The Complete Word Study Dictionary. (Chattanooga, TN, AMG International Inc Revised Edition 1993), e-Sword, Dictionary "allagiasis", G20.

This week, anoint yourself with citrus oil products as it is known for uplifting one's emotions[2]. In this way you are experiencing joy physically and spiritually. Jump, shout and dance for joy!

Going Deeper: Read the following scriptures: Psalm 68:3 Luke 10:21, John 17:13 . Remember that this kind of joy means exuberant action so picture this in your mind as you read these scriptures. What is Holy Spirit revealing to you?

Prayer Time: Ask the Lord to anoint you with the oil of joy and put on some joyful worship music. Begin to dance with Him and let the joy of the Lord fill you.

2 Essential Oils Desk Reference, (Essential Science Publishing, 2006)

Oil of Joy

"...provide for those who grieve... the oil of joy instead of mourning."

(Isaiah 61:3, NIV)

Today we apply the oil of joy deeper into our souls. In Isaiah 61:3, it says that the oil of joy is to replace mourning. Have the Holy Spirit highlight in your soul areas where you are mourning or sad. Ask the Holy Spirit to spiritually rub the oil of joy deep into those places to help you see the events or perceptions from a new perspective of joy. You may need to identify some lies on which you have been feeding, and replace them with God's truth for full freedom of joy. Feel the shift from darkness and sadness to light and joy. Joy brings about a transformation of beauty that others and you can't help but notice. This week give away citrus oil products as a prophetic act of joy overflowing out of your soul. Pray for a deeper realization of God's abundant joy for you and others.

Going Deeper: Read the following scriptures: Psalm 4, Psalm 42, Psalm 51. What is the Lord revealing to you as you read?

Prayer Time: Ask the Lord to reveal the areas of mourning in your heart and release the oil of joy to soothe those memories.

God Rejoicing Over You with Joy

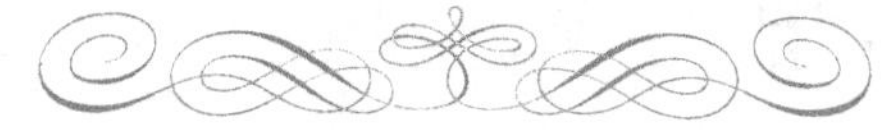

"...He will rejoice (sus) over thee with joy..."

(Zephaniah 3:17, KJV)

The Word Study Dictionary tells us that "rejoice," which is sus in Hebrew, means "exalt, be glad, great rejoicing and jubilant celebration. It describes a horse enjoying his strength (Job 39:21) and the sun joyfully traveling across the sky (Psalm 19:5). These are pictures of how much God rejoices over you with joy."[1] This week delight in joy words from the Bible, soak in joyful worship music, spiritually drink in the beauty of the Holy Spirit or soak in the thought of the cleansing redemption of Jesus. Then, at the end of the week express your thanksgiving and gratefulness of God rejoicing over you with a personal action between you and God that will be a reminder to you in years to come.

---

1 The Word Study Dictionary. (Chattanooga, TN. AMG International Inc., Revised Edition 1993), e-Sword, Dictionary, "Sus", H7797

Going Deeper: Song of Solomon 4:7-15, 6:4-5, Isaiah 62:5. As you read, what is the Lord saying directly to your heart?

Prayer Time: Rejoice in God rejoicing over you!

JOY FEAST

"...He will rejoice over thee with joy (simchah)..."

(Zephaniah 3:17, KJV)

The word joy in this verse is "simchah" in Hebrew and means, "the reality, the experience and manifestation of joy and gladness. It refers to a celebration of something with joyful and cheerful activities like feasting."[1] Ask the Holy Spirit for the reality, experience and manifestation of His joy in you. As he brings you revelation of His joy in you, write it down or share it with a friend. This week, celebrate God's joy in you with a joy feast! Choose foods that have joyful meaning and invite close friends or family that will join in!

Going Deeper: Psalm 4:7, Jeremiah 31:12-14, Acts 14:17. What is God revealing to your heart as you read?

---

1 The Word Study Dictionary. (Chattanooga, TN. AMG International Inc., Revised Edition 1993), e-Sword, Dictionary, "Simchah", H8057.

Prayer Time: Come into God's presence with joy and singing. Ask Him to reveal a plan to celebrate with others in joy – over a meal, a shared celebration in worship, or a feast set on the table with the Lord as your guest of honor.

God Singing Over You with Joy

"…He will joy (gul) over thee with singing".

(Zephaniah 3:17, KJV)

This kind of joy (gul) according to Strongs Concordance, means "to spin around (under the influence of any violent emotion)."[1] Our God has strong emotions of joy about us. Spiritually bathe in the whirlpool of God's powerful, exuberant joy over you. Embrace this truth that will set you free to rejoice! Ask Holy Spirit for the song (s) that The Trinity is singing over you! If you enjoy a whirlpool bath and have access to one, you might want to enjoy one this week as you listen to the love songs of God over your life.

Going Deeper: Isaiah 55:12, John 15:11, Acts 2:28. What is the Lord saying to you as you read?

---

1 Strong, James, S.T.D., LL.D., Strongs Hebrew and Greek Dictionaries, e-Sword, Dictionary, "Gul", H1523.

Prayer Time: Listen to the Holy Spirit to hear specific song (s) He is singing over your life. Sing that/those songs with Him this week, and together, rejoice in your love for each other.

Kingdom of Joy

"For the kingdom of God is...righteousness, peace and joy in the Holy Spirit."

(Romans 14:17, NIV)

Jesus said that the kingdom of God is within you (Luke 17:21). The Holy Spirit is within you, God is within you and Jesus is within you. You are power packed with JOY! Ask Holy Spirit to fill you with overflowing joy, so that it is contagious. An example of this is when others laugh because you are genuinely, hilariously laughing. There is always a twinkle in God's eye towards you. Discover what tickles God's funny bone this week. Laugh joyfully at what God shows you is fun and funny, and share it with others!

Going Deeper: Psalm 23:5, Proverbs 17:22, Philippians 1:25, 26. What is the Lord saying to you as you read?

Prayer Time: Ask God to open your spiritual eyes and ears to see and hear hilarious JOY all around you that you have never seen or heard before.

GENTLENESS, QUIETNESS

AND MEEKNESS

(IN SCRIPTURE THESE THREE WORDS ARE INTERCHANGEABLE OR COMBINED)

GENTLE JESUS

"Take my yoke upon you and learn from me, for I am gentle and humble in heart, and you will find rest for your souls."

(Matthew 11:29, NIV)

The beauty of gentleness comes straight from Jesus' heart. This gentleness that Jesus has to give you brings peacefulness to your heart in incredible ways. When Jesus deposits His gentleness in your soul, you will find that even when things may be stressful all around you, your soul finds rest in the one who loves you the most. This restful soul will be evident and reflected on your face. Your response to the people around you will be one that is gentle and restful to them. Ask Holy Spirit to take the gentleness from Jesus' heart and apply it to your soul. This week you may want to drink a soothing tea or take a bath with essential oils, such as lavender or chamomile,which are known to be relaxing. As you do this, give thanks to your creator for the beauty of gentleness that he has brought into this world.

Going Deeper: Zechariah 9:9, Luke 8:24, Isaiah 40:11. What insight into God's character and nature is being revealed to you? Understand that you have His character and nature in you, making you absolutely beautiful!

Prayer Time: Give thanks to God for being gentle with you and others. Be specific in your thanksgiving by bringing up particular areas of your life or the lives of others where you have experienced God's gentleness.

Fruit of Gentleness

"But the fruit of the Spirit is...gentleness..."

(Galatians 5:22-23, NIV)

According to the Word Study Dictionary, the fruit of gentleness is "calmness towards God in particular."[1] The beauty of this fruit is the act of love that gentleness expresses toward God. This week dwell on the memories in your life of God's goodness toward you. Reflect on the gentle nature of Jesus, who is the exact representation of God (Hebrews 1:3). Eat fruit that symbolizes gentleness to you and share that fruit with a friend as a prophetic act of worship to God.

Going Deeper: Isaiah 32:17, John 15:4,5, Romans 5:1. What is the Lord saying to you as you read?

---

1 The Word Study Dictionary. (Chattanooga, TN. AMG International Inc., Revised Edition 1993), e-Sword, Dictionary, "Praotes", G4236.

Prayer Time: Listen to your heart to see if you have "Calmness towards God." Ask the Holy Spirit to remove any obstacles between you and God. Open your heart to receive a greater revelation of God's gentleness in you.

Gentle and Quiet Spirit

"Your beauty should not come from outward adornment, such as braided hair and the wearing of gold jewelry and fine clothes. Instead it should be that of your inner self, the unfading beauty of a gentle and quiet spirit, which is of great worth in God's sight. For this is the way the holy women of the past who put their hope in God used to make themselves beautiful..."

(1 Peter 3:3-5a, NIV)

This passage is asking the question: "From where do we get our identity?" Do we get our identity from what we wear and the glory of our clothes and jewelry? This passage indicates we are made beautiful by our hope in God. The one who is confident in herself is the one who does not have to impress others with outward beauty. When we are rightly aligned with our creator we will reflect His Holy Spirit's qualities within us. Our souls will be at rest and peaceful, not striving and stressed. This week wear clothes and jewelry that reflect God's quiet and gentle spirit that is born of knowing who you are in Christ Jesus.

Going Deeper: 2 Corinthians 3:17-18, Colossians 1:27, 1 Peter 3. What is the hope you have in God? How does this make you beautiful?

Prayer Time: Ask Holy Spirit to show you in your mind's eye which spiritual clothes He sees you wearing that make you beautiful to Him and the world. Write down or draw the beautiful spiritual clothing and jewelry that Holy Spirit reveals to you.

___

___

___

___

___

___

___

___

___

___

___

Beautiful Meekness

"For the LORD (takes) pleasure in his people:

He will beautify the meek with salvation."

(Psalm 149:4, KJV)

The Lord takes pleasure in making you look good. Humility and meekness look good on everyone. We especially look good when we take on the character traits of Jesus, our Savior. Humility means knowing you need help and having the grace to receive it. Even Jesus only did what He saw the Father doing (John 5:19).

This week, research what the word "salvation" means. Ask others for help in understanding what "salvation" means, so that you will know how God wants to beautify you. Take pleasure in someone this week by bringing beauty into their lives as a reminder of how much pleasure God takes in you.

Going Deeper: Psalm 25:9, 2 Corinthians 6:2 , James 4:10. What understanding have you received as you read?

Prayer Time: Ask Holy Spirit where you need to ask for help. Then ask Him where you are to receive that help. Ask Him to help you take action on this matter.

Gentle Strength

"... in quietness and trust is your strength..."

(Isaiah 30:15, NIV)

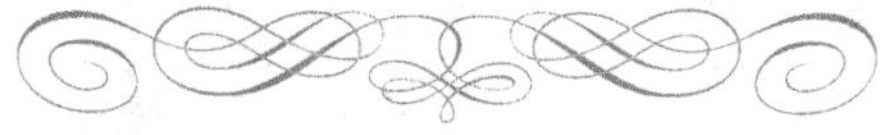

There is a beautiful grace of gentle strength awaiting you. A quiet soul- a soul at rest- is powerful. If you are carrying issues of distrust in your soul, it will rob you of the quietness and strength that God wants to give you. This week, have Holy Spirit show you areas in your soul where you do not trust God or others. If there is any offense in your heart, release the offense to God and ask for His forgiveness to permeate your being. With the help of the Holy Spirit, choose to trust again. Ask Holy Spirit to show you His perspective of safe and perfect trust. Have a trusted friend pray for you in this area.

Going Deeper: Psalm 52:8, Isaiah 26:3-4, Philippians 4:13. What is God saying specifically to your heart as you read?

Prayer Time: Father God wants you to feel safe. Ask Holy Spirit to show you where you do not feel safe and protected. Then ask Holy Spirit to show you in scripture and your mind's eye just how safe you are in Christ Jesus.

Clothing of Gentleness

"Therefore, as God's chosen people, holy and dearly loved, clothe yourselves with compassion, kindness, humility, gentleness and patience."

(Colossians 3:12, NIV)

New clothes! Everyone likes new clothes, especially if they reflect who you are. Gentleness definitely needs to be part of your designer spiritual ensemble.

Let the Holy Spirit enfold you with gentleness this week. As He helps you put it on, you will shine bright and glorious! For fun this week, buy some clothes that represent to you these qualities. If you are on a budget, then have fun going to a thrift store. If God has blessed you with finances, help someone else buy clothes as an act of these virtues.

Going Deeper: Proverbs 31:25, Isaiah 61:10, Galatians 3:27. What did you learn as you read these scriptures?

Prayer Time: Ask Holy Spirit where He wants to go shopping with you and specifically what He wants you to buy to reflect His character and nature. If you need financial resources, ask Father God to provide.

Conspicuous Gentleness

"Let your gentleness be evident to all. The Lord is near."

(Philippians 4:5, NIV)

The Lord is near means that, "He is ready to help, He is at hand."[1] He has given you His gentleness and wants this quality of His in you to be conspicuous. When people think of your personality, they will say that gentleness is a part of your make-up. If you have a personality that is loud, fun and outgoing, your mind may not think that gentleness is a part of your personality. But consider that if your heart is at rest, then being joyful and gentle can work together. After all, Jesus is both joyful and gentle. This week, ask Holy Spirit to open your eyes to the revelation of His gentleness in you so that His gentleness will be evident to yourself! Then ask Holy Spirit whom he would like you to be near,

1 The Word Study Dictionary. (Chattanooga, TN. AMG International Inc., Revised Edition 1993), e-Sword, Dictionary, "Eggus", G1451.

ready to help and give your hand of gentleness as an expression of your love for her/him and God.

Going Deeper: Ephesians 4:2, 1 Corinthians 4:21, 1 Thessalonians 2:7. As you read these scriptures what is revealed to you about God's beautiful nature in you?

Prayer Time: Ask Holy Spirit for creative ideas so that you can bless someone with His gentleness.

Milk

Newborn Faith

"Like newborn babies, crave pure spiritual milk, so that by it you maygrow up in your salvation, now that you have tasted that the Lord is good."

(1 Peter 2:2-3, NIV)

Milk is the first food that you consume when you come into this world. There is a children's song called "Jesus Loves Me," It has been used down through the years to teach children the first and simple truth of God's love for us. Spiritually drink in or bathe in this pure and true thought throughout the week. Use milk beauty products to remind you that the first thing you learn in your newborn faith life is that Jesus Loves You!

Going Deeper: 1 John 3:1, 1 John 4:8-11, John 3:16. What is God saying specifically to your heart as you read?

Prayer Time: Sing "Jesus Loves Me". Then give thanks to God for His love for you. Express your love for Him in prayer or song.

Free Milk

"Come, all you who are thirsty, come to the waters; and you who have no money, come, buy and eat! Come, buy wine and milk without money and without cost."

(Isaiah 55:1, NIV)

Free milk! Jesus paid the price on the cross so that you could have free spiritual milk. There is no cost to this nourishment to your soul. "Jesus loves me this I know" is the first line of the children's song of the previous devotion. How well do you know that Jesus loves you? Ask Holy Spirit to go deeper with the knowledge of His love for you. This week use a milk lotion over your heart and hands as you expect a new revelation of His deep love.

Going Deeper: Psalm 23:6, John 15:13, 1 John 4:14-19. What revelation did you receive in these scriptures?

Prayer Time: Ask Holy Spirit to highlight a scripture for you this week that expresses His deep love for you. Put that scripture in a prominent place and refer to it often.

Sweet Milk

"Your lips drop sweetness as the honeycomb, my bride; milk and honey are under your tongue. The fragrance of your garments is like that of Lebanon."

(Song of Solomon 4:11, NIV)

Beautiful women have beautiful words come from their lips and tongue to bring life, joy and peace. Ask Holy Spirit to fill you with the sweet milk of His words. Then the beauty that God has given you will be shared with others to bring nourishment to their souls. Wear lipstick or lip gloss that shines white as milk, as a reminder or as a witness to others of the beauty of sweet words from heaven inside of you that must be released to the world!

Going Deeper: Proverbs 24:26, Proverbs 25:11, Proverbs 15:23. What is God highlighting to you in these scriptures? What steps can you take to apply them?

Prayer Time: Ask Holy Spirit for specific words of beauty to share with others.

Simple Pleasures

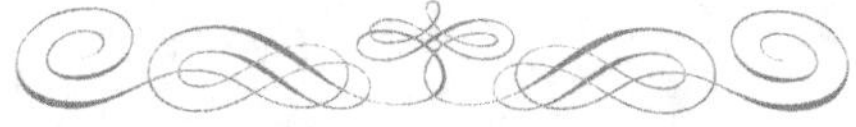

"If the LORD is pleased with us, He will lead us into that land, a land flowing with milk and honey, and will give it to us."

(Numbers 14:8, NIV)

A land flowing with milk and honey does not just mean a land filled with cows and bees. It means plenty of rich green pasture, a variety of bright flowers and fruit trees to delight the cows and bees! Our God is a generous God, and He wants to bring nourishment to our souls in so many ways. Take nature walks this week and ask Holy Spirit to bring to your mind simple truths that will bring more beauty to your soul. God loves to talk to us through nature (Romans 1:20). Especially notice the abundance of simple pleasures that are sweet and nourishing to the soul. Write them down in a journal to bring nourishment to your soul at a future date.

Going Deeper: Psalm 8, Psalm 23, Luke 12:22-32. What nourishes your soul in these scriptures?

Prayer Time: Give thanks to God for specific simple pleasures you experience this week.

Inner Landscape

"...a land flowing with milk and honey, the most beautiful of all land..."

(Ezekiel 20:15, NIV)

Do you have a good inner atmosphere to soak in God's beauty? Ask Holy Spirit if there is anything in your heart or mind that clutters your spiritual landscape. Then make a trade with Him for a beautiful mindset or attitude to replace what is not so beautiful. Ahh...that feels better. Spiritually soak in the new beauty within. Apply a milk face mask this week to remind you of God's cleansing power in your life.

Going Deeper: John 1:9, Acts 24:16, Hebrew 10:22-23. As you read, how is God revealing His love toward you?

Prayer Time: Give thanks to the Holy Spirit for His cleansing qualities in your soul. Revel in the feeling of a clean soul.

GOOD MILK

"In that day the mountains will drip new wine, and the hills will flow with milk..."

(Joel 3:18, NIV)

What is flowing out of your life? Whatever we drink or feed on spiritually for our souls will flow out of our lives. Is there spiritual or physical junk food or drinks that need to be cut out of your life for more beauty to flow? Ask Holy Spirit to fill up your soul and body with self-control and good things from His table. This week drink or eat healthy milk products. If you cannot digest cow's milk because of health problems, use an alternative milk product. As you drink or eat these carefully chosen foods and drinks focus on God's goodness in you, around you, and upon you.

Going Deeper: Psalm 19:8, Matthew 10:8b, Luke 6:45. What did you learn in these scriptures? How can you apply what you learned?

Prayer Time: Ask Holy Spirit to reveal unhealthy spiritual food that you have been eating that needs to be cut out. Then ask Him to show you where to go to get healthy spiritual food. Give thanks to God for the abundance of healthy spiritual food and drink that He has or will supply for you.

Pure Adoration

"His eyes are like doves by the water streams, washed in milk, mounted like jewels."

(Song of Solomon 5:12, NIV)

Jesus looks at you with eyes of purity and adores you! Spiritually drink in this thought and bathe in His love and adoration for you. As you physically shower or bathe this week, be reminded that all your sins are washed away through Jesus' sacrifice. You may want to take a milk bath to remind you of the purity of this truth.

When you see doves, water streams, milk and jewels this week, let them be a reminder that God's eyes of love are upon you, delighting in you! You are altogether lovely to Him.

Going Deeper: Psalm 45:11, Song of Solomon 1:15, Jeremiah 31:3. As you read, what is the Lord saying directly to your heart? Treasure what He is saying to you.

Prayer Time: Ask Holy Spirit to give you a picture in your mind's eye of how God sees you as His beautiful one that He adores.

Spiritual Cleanse

Preparing for Cleansing

"Cleanse me with hyssop, and I will be clean; wash me, and I will be whiter than snow."

(Psalm 51:7, NIV)

Cleansing is always a part of becoming more beautiful. Whether it is cleansing our skin or going through a fast to cleanse the bodily system to rid ourselves of toxins, we will feel better and look more beautiful when we remove impurities. This week ask Holy Spirit to prepare you for a spiritual cleanse. The greatest preparation is to know in your mind and heart that Jesus loves you and wants the best for you. He wants to free you from anything that may hinder the beauty inside of you from shining forth. Ask Holy Spirit to sustain you in this cleansing time (Psalm 51: 12). Consciously use a skin cleanser or carefully choose a fast that will benefit your body. As you go through this process, ask Holy Spirit to help you develop a good attitude towards cleansing body and soul.

Going Deeper: Psalm 24:3-6, Psalm 51, Luke 5:12-13. How is Jesus communicating His love for you in these scriptures?

Prayer Time: Ask Holy Spirit if there is any resistance in your soul to a spiritual cleanse. Then ask him to remove any obstacles so that you can become as beautiful as you were meant to be.

Cleansing from a Guilty Conscience

"...let us draw near to God with a sincere heart in full assurance of faith, having our hearts sprinkled to cleanse us from a guilty conscience and having our bodies washed with pure water."

(Hebrews 10:22, NIV)

One of the things that mars beauty is a guilty conscience. Jesus does not want you to carry any guilt, and so He became a guilt offering for you.[1] Ask Holy Spirit to show you any guilt in your soul that you need to give to Jesus.

After you have given Him the guilt, ask Holy Spirit what Jesus is giving you in exchange for the guilt. Jesus will give you a character quality of Himself that will be good and healing to your soul. A clear conscience always feels good! This week take a cleansing bath with one of the following: Epsom

1 Read Hebrews 10 NIV for reference of Jesus becoming our guilt offering.

salts, apple cider vinegar, ginger root, baking soda, oatmeal or herbal tea. Do some homework to determine which of these would work best for you.

Going Deeper: Isaiah 53:10-11, Ephesians 5:1-2, Hebrews 10. How is Jesus communicating His love for you in these scriptures?

Prayer Time: Give thanks to Jesus for becoming a guilt offering for you so that you do not have to carry any guilt whatsoever! If there is an action that you need to take to make restoration with another, ask Holy Spirit to help you do what needs to be done. Be sure and rejoice in a guilt-free conscience. God loves to see his daughters celebrate their freedom!

Cleansed from Sin

"If we confess our sins, he is faithful and just and will forgive us our sins and purify us from all unrighteousness."

(1John 1:9, NIV)

When we carry un-confessed sins, they weigh us down, and this unnecessary weight is reflected on our faces and in our demeanor. As is often quoted, "confession is good for the soul." When we confess to God our sins and He purifies us from all unrighteousness (things that are not right), our hearts and countenance are lighter and happier. We were made to be free from sin! Ask Holy Spirit to reveal any sin that needs to be confessed. Then confess and ask Holy Spirit to break any sin pattern that is destructive to the beautiful you that is waiting to shine forth. This week, carefully choose aerobic exercises to match your specific physical condition. Work up a sweat and focus diligently on losing some calories and excess weight if needed. This exercise will be a sign to you that God is working all things together for good in your life (Romans 8:28).

Going Deeper: Psalm 139:23-24, Isaiah 1:18, John 3:17. How is Jesus communicating His love for you in these scriptures?

Prayer Time: Give thanks to God for the beautiful gift of confession and His great love for you. Thank Him that when you confess your sin that He does not condemn but rather gives you His abundant forgiveness and love.

Healthy Cleanse

"How much more, then, will the blood of Christ, who through the eternal Spirit offered himself unblemished to God, cleanse our consciences from acts that lead to death, so that we may serve the living God!"

(Hebrews 9:14, NIV)

Not only does God want to cleanse our consciences from guilt but He wants to deliver us from acts that lead to death! There are thought patterns and actions that diminish our health and beauty. God wants us to be free from these things! Ask Holy Spirit to reveal any thought patterns or actions that are depleting your beauty and ask Him to break these negative patterns. Take action this week to break any unhealthy patterns and start healthy ones. Take walks, jogs or runs this week to remind you what unhealthy patterns you are walking/running away from and what healthy patterns you are walking/running towards.

Going Deeper: Romans 12:2, 2 Corinthians 7:1, 2 Timothy 2:22. How is Jesus communicating His love for you in these scriptures?

Prayer Time: Ask God for an accountability partner to help you break any unhealthy patterns. Ask God for His strength and courage.

PURE LIPS

"Then will I purify the lips of the peoples, that all of them may call on the name of the LORD and serve him shoulder to shoulder."

(Zephaniah 3:9, NIV)

God wants you to call upon Him! He is the one that purifies our lips so that we know how to pray. When we are in agreement with God and others about how we can serve this world, it is a beautiful thing to behold. This week, ask God what is on his heart for you to pray. Get together with others and listen for specific directions from God to bring beauty to this world. Then work shoulder- to-shoulder to bring it about. There is so much joy in working together with God and others to bring heaven's goodness to others.

Going Deeper: 1 Corinthians 3:9, 2 Corinthians 6:1-2, Philippians 4:3. What is the Holy Spirit highlighting to you in these scriptures?

Prayer Time: Ask Holy Spirit to show you how Father God sees your words of prayer and praise. Draw a picture or write about what He shows you.

PURE HOPE

"...But we know that when he appears, we shall be like him, for we shall see him as he is. Everyone who has this hope in him purifies himself, just as he is pure."

(1 John 3:2b-3, NIV)

Have you ever thought of hope being a purifying agent? Hope brings life, excitement and joy. The great hope in this scripture is that we will be like Jesus and see Him as He really is. Ask Holy Spirit to cleanse any hopelessness out of your soul and to replace it with the hope of Christ Jesus as a permanent fixture. Your eyes will express the bright beauty of this hope. Ask Holy Spirit to open your eyes to see Jesus, "the hope of glory,"[1] like you have never seen Him before. This week, try new eye shadow, eyeliner or any beautifying eye products to remind you of your new outlook on life.

---

1 Colossians 1:27 NIV

Going Deeper: Romans 5:1-2, Ephesians 1:18, 2 Thessalonians 2:16-17. How is Jesus communicating His love for you in these scriptures?

Prayer Time: Ask Holy Spirit to show you what thoughts you have been focusing on that bring hopelessness in your life. Ask Him to redirect your mind to thoughts of hope and purpose. A definition of hope is: the expectation of something good.

Beautiful Thoughts

"Finally, brothers and sisters, whatever is true, whatever is noble, whatever is right, whatever is pure, whatever is lovely, whatever is admirable—if anything is excellent or praiseworthy—think about such things."
(Philippians 4:8, NIV)

Now that you have gone through a week of spiritual cleansing, it is time to fill yourself with beauty. Beauty starts with our thoughts that turn into beliefs that turn into actions, which turn into behaviors, that turn into habits, which turn into character, that takes us to our destinies. This week, soak in beautiful thoughts that are true, noble, right, pure, lovely, admirable, excellent, and praiseworthy. Spiritually drink in or notice words that are spoken to you that are on this list. Ask Holy Spirit to help develop the habit of dwelling on beautiful thoughts that become a part of your beautiful character that will take you to your destiny. This week carefully choose music to listen to that has beautiful words that encourage you to think beautiful thoughts.

Going Deeper: Psalm 100:5, Psalm 23:6, Psalm 103:1-6. How is Jesus communicating His love for you in these scriptures?

Prayer Time: Listen to music that inspires you, and speak out loud words that the Holy Spirit gives you that will take you to your beautiful destiny.

Honey Cleanse

Sweet Words

***"Pleasant words are a honeycomb, sweet to the soul and healing to the bones."* (Proverbs 16:24, NIV)**

We have looked at our words and how they affect others. Now let us look at how words from others affect our beauty. Not all words spoken to us or written on a page bring life and beauty to our souls and bodies. We have the power of choice to savor words that enhance our beauty within and without. This week, be aware of words that are sweet. Write them down and meditate on them. Don't receive or dwell on words that are not life giving. Give all unhealthy words spoken to you this week to Jesus and ask Holy Spirit to highlight words of life for you to chew on and digest and bring a life of sweet beauty.

Eat honey this week to remind you of sweet words of love, grace, comfort and joy. You may even want to get a honeycomb just for fun.

Going Deeper: Psalm 48:9, Proverbs 4, John 6:27,63. What beautiful words are being spoken to you through the Holy Spirit in these scriptures?

Prayer Time: Ask Holy Spirit for the specific words He wants you to focus on for your life. Ask Him to show you creative ways to place these words in your life so they are conspicuous to you every day.

God's Words are Sweet

"How sweet are your words to my taste, sweeter than honey to my mouth!"

(Psalm 119:103, NIV)

The Psalmist is speaking of God's words to us. As you read the Bible this week ask Holy Spirit to quicken His words in your soul. This will begin the process of God bringing more of His life and beauty to you. Meditate on the love and joy God has in you. There is nothing quite like being loved to bring out radiance in a loved one. Use honey lip products this week: balm, gloss, scrub, and lipstick as a reminder of the sweetness of God's word on your lips and in your mouth. Share these sweet words with others as you are given opportunity.

Going Deeper: Psalm 119:105, Matthew 4:4, 2 Peter 1:19. As you read, what is the Lord revealing to you?

Prayer Time: Ask Holy Spirit for a specific Bible verse to share with a specific person. Ask for a creative way to share this life giving word.

SWEET WISDOM

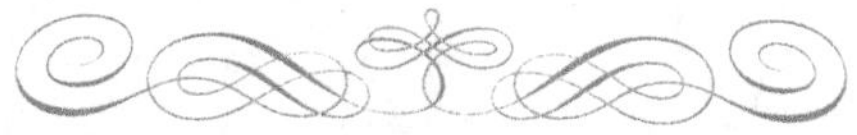

"Know also that wisdom is like honey for you: If you find it, there is a future hope for you, and your hope will not be cut off."

(Proverbs 24:14, NIV)

Wisdom is sweet! It brings you hope. Hope is a vital ingredient to a beautiful countenance. Hope is looking forward to good things. What good thing are you looking forward to? Ask Holy Spirit for wisdom on how to attain what you hope for. Enjoy the sweetness of your life! Hopelessness means you have less hope. Most likely you are looking through the dark glasses of fear and anxiety if you are struggling with hopelessness. Searching for wisdom is like looking for precious treasure. God loves to give you His perspective on your situation. This week, ask for God's perspective and His wisdom. Rejoice in the sweetness of this wisdom. Apply a honey face mask this week for the fun of it and for the joy of knowing that God is giving you a facelift with hope and wisdom.

Going Deeper: Colossians 2:2-3, James1:5, James 3:17. How is Holy Spirit encouraging you in these scriptures?

Prayer Time: Ask for wisdom in a specific area of your life and expect God to give it to you. Write down the wisdom He gives you and rejoice in God's goodness to you!

SWEET IDENTITY

"It is not good to eat too much honey, nor is it honorable to seek one's own honor."

(Proverbs 25:27)

On the surface, this verse looks like it is talking about self-control. We all know about not eating too many sweets. We also know how unlovely it is for someone to push themselves into a place of honor. But what if this verse is not only about self-control but also about our self-image? What we believe about ourselves will either drive us into insecurity or enable us to be all that we can be (secure in knowing who I am). Find your security in who God says you are. Ask Holy Spirit to reveal to you what ingredients he has placed in your life to make you into the beautiful woman that He has in His mind. This week make a game of saying "no" to sweets that you don't need. Joke about it with your friends and family. Have fun! This week, use a honey body scrub or honey body wash knowing that your security in your identity is wrapped up in the sweetness of God's love for you.

Going Deeper: Deuteronomy 33:12, Psalm 16:5-6, 2 Corinthians 5:17. What feelings are stirred up in these scriptures? Why?

Prayer Time: Ask Holy Spirit for a new enjoyment of self-control. Give thanks to God for this part of His nature that He shares with you. Rejoice that you are made in the image of God!

Sweet Appetite

"One who is full loathes honey from the comb, but to the hungry even what is bitter tastes sweet."

(Proverbs 27:7, NIV)

How is your appetite for life? Are you hungry for better or best? How strong is that desire to lose weight or exercise, so that you look and feel your best? What is your motivation? Where is your daily focus? Who is encouraging you to reach your goal? What are you craving? Why? What belief is it, that is deep within you, that is strong enough to help you reach your goal? What belief in you is hindering you from reaching your goal? Write out the answers to these questions in a journal. Ask Holy Spirit to assist you in breaking out of mediocrity, and develop a healthy hunger for better and best in all areas of life. This week, use a honey foot soak, scrub or bath and realize that God is cleansing your thoughts and beliefs that have led you into the land of mediocrity. At the same time, you can recognize where God is leading you into new opportunities of beauty.

Going Deeper: Psalm 18:32, Ephesians 3:16, Philippians 4:13. How is Jesus revealing His love for you in these scriptures?

Prayer Time: Ask Holy Spirit to help you identify beliefs that are hindering you from becoming more beautiful inside and out. Then ask Him to replace negative beliefs with positive ones that are God given.

Royal Honey

"...Your food was honey, olive oil and the finest flour. You became very beautiful, and rose to be a queen." (Ezekiel 16:13, NIV)

Honey is the food of queens! Sweet to the taste and mixed with the finest ingredients, it becomes a rich, royal delight. You are becoming very beautiful and rising in your royalty. Your words are sweeter and your countenance is brighter. Consider today how much you have changed in the past weeks and months. Rejoice in who you are becoming! Give thanks to God for creating you and developing you into beautiful royalty! Rise up to your position in Christ Jesus. You are a woman of honor and integrity. Feel the authority that God has given you to say "No" to the base things in this world. This week enjoy a special treat made with honey. Say "No" to too much honey-laden goodies, but say "Yes" to enjoy the perfect amount to bring fullness of joy.

Going Deeper: Psalm 45:9-11, Isaiah 62:5, 1 Peter 2:9. How is God expressing His joy of you in these scriptures?

Prayer Time: Ask Holy Spirit to help you to feel the joy of the perfect amount of sweetness in your life. Ask Him to show you how you have progressed from beauty to more beauty in your life.

Lovely Honey

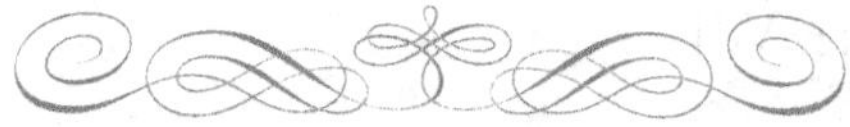

"I have come into my garden, my sister, my bride... I have eaten my honeycomb and my honey; I have drunk my wine and my milk. Eat, friends, and drink; drink your fill of love."

(Song of Solomon 5:1, TNIV)

When we are full of love, we are sweet to others. God is Love (1 John 4:8). Go to the source of love today and enjoy the sweetness of His love for you and your love for Him. Spend time with Him whether indoors or outdoors in whatever way you choose. Meditate on all the love in your life. Bring to your mind memories that are filled with feelings of love. Write letters, notes, emails or texts of love this week to those who have shown you what true love is. Use honey products this week and give them away to others as a symbol of the love that you have received and the joy of the overflow in your beautiful life.

Going Deeper: 1 Corinthians 13, Ephesians 3, 1 John 4. What scriptures are highlighted by the Holy Spirit? Why?

Prayer Time: Ask Holy Spirit to show you specific people that have shown you what God's love looks like. Give thanks to God for those people and bless them.

Perfume and Incense

Cleanse

Beautiful Friends

"Perfume and incense bring joy to your heart. And a friend is sweeter when he gives you honest advice."

(Proverbs 27:9, NIV)

Studies of perfumes and incense have indicated that they can provoke strong emotions.[1] It depends, however, upon the kind of perfume or incense whether it brings about good emotions or dark emotions. So, too, our choice of friends will bring more beauty of soul and character or detract from the beauty within and without. Choose wisely with whom you associate and from whom you receive counsel. Spend time this week with friends who bring out the best in you! Give a friend a perfume or incense that reminds you of her and tell her

1 Essential Oils Desk Reference, (Essential Science Publishing, 2006) 8

how much you appreciate her. Maybe go perfume shopping or sampling with her.

Going Deeper: Psalm 1, Proverbs 17:17, Proverbs 18:24. How do these scriptures bring life and joy into your life?

Prayer Time: Give thanks to God for the friends in your life that bring out the best in you! Pour out blessings upon them in prayer. Let them know of your appreciation of them in your life.

Beautiful Name

"Pleasing is the fragrance of your perfumes; your name is like perfume poured out..." Ecclesiastes 7:1 "A good name is better than fine perfume..."

(Song of Solomon 1:3, NIV)

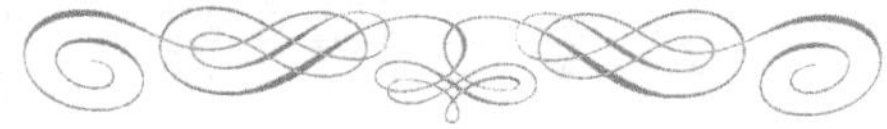

Do you consider your name beautiful? Why or why not? We can make our names a sweet aroma by the beauty of God's character and nature in us. Ask each person of the Trinity, (Father, Son and Holy Spirit) what each one thinks when He hears your name. Renounce any unlovely thoughts about your name and ask Holy Spirit to bring Jesus' life to it, so that the fragrance of your name brings life to yourself and others! If there are areas in your life that need adjusting so that your name, when heard, brings honor, ask Holy Spirit to help you with the necessary changes that need to be made. Wear perfume this week that reminds you that God loves to say your name.

Going Deeper: Proverbs 3:3-4, Proverbs 22:1, Revelation 2:17. How is Jesus expressing His love for you in these scriptures?

Prayer Time: Ask Holy Spirit to help you to creatively enjoy your name. Look up the meaning of your name. Consider having your name displayed as a painting or drawing. Redeem it from any darkness and bring it out to shine brightly!

Perfume of Character

"While the king was at his table, my perfume spread its fragrance."

(Song of Solomon 1:12 NIV)

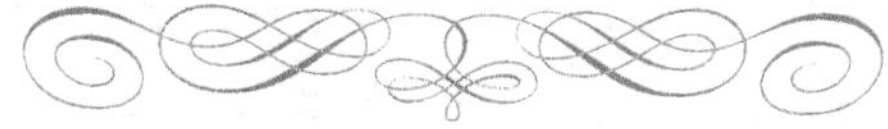

We all carry a presence of who we are, wherever we go. Before we enter a room, if people are talking about us, the fragrance of who we are precedes us. What we focus on will determine our fragrance. If we are focused on joy, delight and goodness, then these things will precede us into a room, or at least linger after we have left. If we focus on complaints, problems and discouragement, then this fragrance will linger in people's minds about us. Where is your focus? What are you spreading? Ask Holy Spirit to bring about the right chemistry in your persona for a perfume of beauty to precede you wherever you go. If He says He already loves your perfume of character and beauty, give thanks and rejoice, you can always ask for more! Wear a perfume this week to bring you joy and to remind you to be a carrier of joy!

Going Deeper: 2 Corinthians 2:14, 2 Corinthians 4:8, Hebrews 12:2. As you read, what is the Lord saying directly to your heart?

Prayer Time: Ask Holy Spirit if there is anything that you are focusing on that needs a shift. Then ask Holy Spirit to help you to develop a beautiful focus that remains as a part of your character.

LAVISH LOVE

"A woman came to him with an alabaster jar of very expensive perfume, which she poured on his head as he was reclining at the table."

(Matthew 26:7, NIV)

This verse is about giving honor and not counting the cost. The woman in this passage of scripture showed that she valued Jesus above money or her reputation. When she went into the room, she most likely knew she would be judged. She considered Jesus worth the cost. Jesus would have carried the fragrance of her perfume and her act of honor to the cross. It would have been a comfort to him as he got a whiff of the fragrance still lingering on his hair and head.[1] A huge part of beauty is lavish love. Ask Holy Spirit how you can lavish love on people this week and leave a lingering fragrance

---

1 Sermon from Bethel School of the Supernatural Student February 2012.

on their souls. Give away a perfume or lotion as a reminder to someone of your love for him or her.

Going Deeper: Matthew 25:40, Mark 12:30-31, John 15:12-13. How is Jesus expressing His love to you in these scriptures?

Prayer Time: Ask Holy Spirit to remind you of a time in your life where God lavished His love on you. Give thanks to God for His great love for you.

Fragrance of Gratefulness

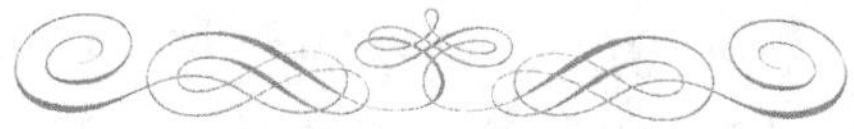

"Then Mary took about a pint of pure nard, an expensive perfume; she poured it on Jesus' feet and wiped his feet with her hair. And the house was filled with the fragrance of the perfume."

(John 12:3, NIV)

A dinner was being given at Mary's house in honor of Jesus. Lazarus, Mary's brother, had been raised from the dead by Jesus just a short while before this dinner. Mary must have sat at Jesus' feet many times before the resurrection of her brother, but this was different. Her life had been forever changed, having had first-hand experience of the love and power of Jesus for her family. Her heart was filled with gratefulness, and she needed to express her gratefulness by pouring out expensive perfume and washing Jesus' feet. Everyone was aware of her love for Jesus because "the house was filled with the fragrance of the perfume."[1] A grateful heart is a thing of great beauty to God and to others. Ask

1 John 12:3 NIV

Holy Spirit to bring to your mind where you have first-hand experience of God's love and power in your life. Then pour out the fragrance of your gratefulness to God in an extravagant way that fills the environment around you with its aroma of beauty and love.

Going Deeper: Psalm 50:23, Luke 10:38-42, John 12:1-8. What is the Holy Spirit highlighting for you in these scriptures? Why?

Prayer Time: Ask Holy Spirit to remind you of a time where God's power in your life was transformational. Express your gratefulness to God in praise and thanksgiving.

Perfume of Life

"Because of Christ, we give off a sweet scent rising to God, which is recognized by those on the way of salvation--an aroma redolent with life."

(2 Corinthians 2:15, The Message)

The source of all beauty is Jesus Christ. He is the best perfume that one could wear. The fragrance of His perfume gives life! When you hang out with Jesus, you catch his scent of life and give it away unconsciously. Every time you look at the time of day today, turn your mind to Jesus and be aware of soaking up His perfume of life. Be conscious of the effect of the aroma of life filling the atmosphere around you. Notice the beauty of life all around you and express the beauty of it through words, or a dance, a song, an art piece or a shout. Be sure and smell the perfume of flowers this week as a reminder of the beauty of life. Give flowers away as a prophetic sign of spreading the aroma of Christ Jesus to the world.

Going Deeper: Isaiah 53, John 15:1-17, John 20. How is Jesus expressing His love for you in these scriptures?

Prayer Time: Ask Holy Spirit to bring to mind scents that bring life, light and joy to your soul every time you smell them. Give thanks to Jesus for the aroma of life in you and around you.

INCENSE OF PRAYER

"And when he had taken it, the four living creatures and the twenty-four elders fell down before the Lamb. Each one had a harp and they were holding golden bowls full of incense, which are the prayers of the saints."

(Revelation 5:8 NIV)

Our prayers are sweet incense to God and for others. Our prayers of praise, worship, thanksgiving, intercession and supplication soar to heaven and the answers to our prayers are then sent back to earth to create beauty all around us. You release that beauty when you partner with the Holy Spirit in prayer for what is on His heart and your heart. Ask Holy Spirit what is on His heart that will create beauty in you and in others. Write down what you hear and pray accordingly as sweet incense that will spread its influence in heaven and on earth. Do this several times throughout the week, creating aromas mingling together as a powerful force of beauty within and without. You may want to burn some incense or light a fragrant candle this week as a reminder to pray.

Going Deeper: Luke 17:21, Philippians 4:6, 1 Thessalonians 5:16-18. As you read, what is the Lord saying directly to your heart?

Prayer Time: Ask Holy Spirit what prayer of beauty He would have you pray this week.

Plant Life

Myrrh

"The time of beauty treatment was spent as follows: six months using oil of myrrh..." (Esther 2:12, NIV)

Myrrh is used in the Bible as a beautiful fragrance of lovers (Song of Solomon 1:13), It was used in the sacred anointing oil (Exodus 30:23), it was given as a gift to baby Jesus (Matthew 2:11) and it was used at Jesus' death and burial (Mark 15:23, John 19:39). Most likely Esther used it for its properties of giving beautiful skin. But we can see from scripture that God has used this oil for meaningful purposes. It is a symbol of love, holy anointing, new life and death. This week use oil of myrrh or myrrh soap and ask Holy Spirit to show areas of your life where he has placed deep into your soul His qualities of love, holy anointing and the death of something that brings new life. Journal these areas and share what you discovered with a friend.

Then give thanks to God that the beauty He has placed in you is deeper than skin deep.

Going Deeper: John 5:24, 2 Corinthians 1:21-22, Ephesians 3:16-19. What new revelation is God showing you in these scriptures?

Prayer Time: Give thanks to God for the different facets of beauty He has created in you.

OLIVE OIL

"They also brought spices and olive oil for the light and for the anointing oil and for the fragrant incense." (Exodus 35:28, NIV)

Olive oil is used in scripture for the fuel for lamps to produce light. It is used for anointing kings, priests, sacred items, and people for consecration and for healing. It is used in the sacred incense rising up to God. It is packed with meaning and usefulness, as are you in God's sight. When we know that we are created with purpose and power to bless God and others, it affects our demeanor and the beauty of our stature. Are you filled with the knowledge of the light you produce in this world? Do you know your purpose and assignments to bless God and others? Ask Holy Spirit to reveal to you the unique light you bring to the world. Ask Him what anointing(s) you have that empower others and bring beauty to this earth. Give away what you have and it will be multiplied many times over. This week, use olive oil beauty products or cook with olive oil to remind you of the lasting beauty that you bring to this world through the power of the Holy Spirit.

Going Deeper: Job 29:6, Psalm 23:5, Matthew 5:14-16. What revelation is God giving you in these scriptures?

Prayer Time: Give thanks to God for the light He has given you to share with others. Ask Holy Spirit to set up divine appointments so that you can give it away.

FRANKINCENSE

"And when they were come into the house, they saw the young child with Mary his mother, and fell down, and worshipped him: and when they had opened their treasures, they presented unto him gifts; gold, and frankincense, and myrrh."

(Matthew 2:11, NIV)

The best frankincense is a translucent resin that has no blemishes. It can be burned as incense or used as an essential oil. It is said to have many healing properties and heightens spiritual awareness. [1] There are certain influences, such as frankincense, in this world that bring healing to our souls, minds and bodies. There are also certain environments and activities that heighten our spiritual awareness. When we go out of our way, as the wise men did when looking for the Christ child, to seek closeness with Jesus, it is a treasure given to him. Make a deliberate choice this week

1 Wikipedia.org/wiki/frankincense (accessed February 22, 2013).

to place yourself in environments that heighten your spiritual awareness of Jesus. As you do this, look for a healing effect as well. Being in the right place at the right time for the right reason brings a sense of balance and grounding to our souls. Look for frankincense products this week and use them as a reminder of the treasure that Jesus is to you and the world.

Going Deeper: Exodus 30:34-36, Song of Solomon 4:6-7, Matthew 6:21. How is God expressing His delight in you personally through these scriptures?

Prayer Time: Ask Holy Spirit to show you the best environment that will promote your spiritual growth in Christ Jesus. Then ask Him to give you a first step to take towards being in that environment on a regular basis.

Aloes

"All your robes are fragrant with myrrh and aloes and cassia; from palaces adorned with ivory the music of the strings makes you glad."

(Psalm 45:8, NIV)

You are the fragrance of royalty! Because of your position in Christ, you know who you are. You have a family likeness with your creator. You have inherited grace and favor which brings you a strong sense of belonging. There is great beauty in the family of God. It is time to celebrate that beauty! All week long, rejoice in the beauty of your family. Tell them the beauty that you see in them. Do not go fishing for compliments, but if they come your way, write them down and savor them. Use aloe products this week and give them away to members of your royal family. Be sure and wrap these gifts with joy and love.

Going Deeper: Numbers 24:5-6, John 1:12-13, 1 John 3:2. What is God revealing to you in these scriptures?

Prayer Time: Ask Holy Spirit to give you creative ideas to bless your family this week.

Rose of Sharon & Lily of the Valley

"I am a rose of Sharon, a lily of the valleys. Like a lily among thorns is my darling among the maidens." (Song of Songs 2:1, 2, NIV)

Every woman loves flowers, and each flower has its own unique beauty. We love the colors, fragrance, intricacy and delicate nature of flowers. Each woman has a unique beauty all her own, in many ways similar to the nature of flowers. Notice in the verse above that it speaks of a lily among thorns. We know that lilies do not have thorns, so this may mean that the lily is in the midst of brambles or sticker bushes.[1] When we know who we are in all our unique glory, we can be in a hostile environment and still shine with the glorious beauty that God gave each one of us. God and others then see the contrast and are enthralled by you being you. This week, ask the Holy Spirit to share with you the

1 Johann (C.F.) Keil and Franz Delitzsch, Keil & Delitzsch Commentary on the Old Testament, e-Sword, Commentary, Song of Songs 2:2.

truth of your intricate, delicate, fragrant, colorful character and nature that He created. Write these beautiful qualities down and meditate/soak in the beauty of who God created you to be, and rejoice! Buy, pick, find a picture or draw a flower today that you feel best represents the beauty within you, so that every time you look at it, you can be encouraged.

Going Deeper: Song of Solomon 2:10-13, Song of Solomon 4:9-16, Song of Solomon 6:2-3. As you read, what is the Lord saying directly to your heart?

Prayer Time: Give thanks to God for the unique beauty He created in you. Ask Holy Spirit for a deeper awareness of your unique beauty.

FRUIT

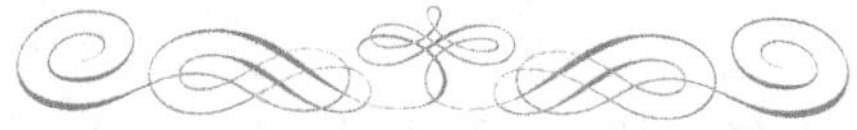

"The fig tree forms its early fruit; the blossoming vines spread their fragrance. Arise, come, my darling; my beautiful one, come with me."

(Song of Songs 2:13, NIV)

Spring is a time of new beginnings, where the fragrance of the fruit blossom hints of the fruit to come that refreshes. There are places in our lives where we do not have the full fruit of beauty, but we can detect the beginnings of new life and fruitfulness. There is a special beauty to this time. Enjoy the process of becoming more beautiful. Celebrate new beginnings this week. Ask a good friend to share with you an area where he or she sees a new beauty that is forming in you. Ask Holy Spirit to confirm it in you. Then cultivate that new life by giving it the proper light/revelation from God, soil/good environment, rain/heaven drenched moments and nutrients/words that inspire. Make purposeful choices that bring out this new beauty that is emerging with the strength and power of the Lord. Eat fruit or use fruit beauty products that represent this blossoming beauty in you.

Going Deeper: Jeremiah 17:7-8, Mark 4:26-29, John 15;1-11. What is God saying specifically to your heart as you read?

Prayer Time: Ask God for specific spiritual fruit in your life. Ask him to show you how to cultivate this fruit while it is being developed.

Tree of Life

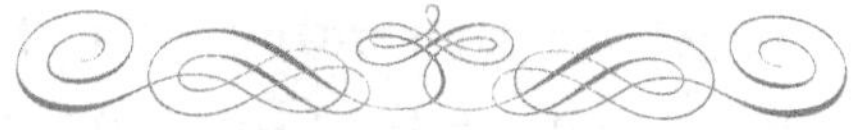

"Wisdom is a life-giving tree, the source of happiness for all who hold on to her."

(Proverbs 3:18, CEV)

A woman may be beautiful in form and face, but foolishness and lack of discretion can severely damage her beauty. The word "wisdom" in this passage means: "(in a good sense) skillful, wisdom, wisely and wit."[1] Each word we speak has a value and timing to it that brings greater beauty and life when we say the right word(s) at the right time. If we have a sense of humor (wit) and make others laugh, we increase our beauty to the Lord, others and ourselves because there is great enjoyment. When we can give wise counsel, have discretion, understanding and insight, we enhance the beauty in this world. The skills that God has given us, and which we have developed, bring much joyous

---

1 Strong, James, S.T.D., LL.D., Strongs Hebrew and Greek Dictionaries, e-Sword, Dictionary,"Chokmah", H2451

life and beauty as we use them for others. This week, use aromatic wood beauty products and breathe the fragrance to remind you that wisdom is a life-giving tree. Ask God for wisdom in specific areas of your life, so that you will find the source of happiness and hold onto it! Take notice of wisdom bringing beauty and life to yourself and others.

Going Deeper: Proverbs 8:11, Proverbs 11:22, James 1:5. What is God saying specifically to your heart as you read?

Prayer Time: Ask for wisdom from the Holy Spirit in a specific area of your life. Write down what you receive and then read it often.

THE BODY

MOUTH/LIPS

"Your lips are like a scarlet ribbon; your mouth is lovely..."
(Song of Solomon 4:3, NIV)

Our mouths are most beautiful when we use them in a smile. There are many ways to smile: a full on laugh, a coy smile, a pouty smile, a mischievous smile, an inviting smile, a smile full of kindness, a gentle smile, etc. Practice smiles in the mirror and find the ones that bring out the most beauty from the inside out. Give them away. Take pictures of yourself smiling to remember the beauty of the moment. This week, wear lip gloss or lipstick to remind you of the beauty of the lips that God gave you. Give away pure and beautiful kisses.

Going Deeper: Psalm 141:3, Proverbs 23:16, Proverbs 24:26. What is God revealing to you about your mouth or lips in these scriptures?

Prayer Time: Ask Holy Spirit to fill you so full of His joy that you smile often without even thinking about it. Give thanks for every smile that comes your way this week.

Hair

***"... Your hair is like royal tapestry; the king is held captive by its tresses."* **

(Song of Solomon 7:5, NIV)

Do you like your hair? Do you like the color and the style? Do you feel attractive because of your hair? This verse is saying the king can't keep his eyes off of his woman. One of the ingredients of beauty is attractiveness. Women were made to attract and capture with their beauty. Your hairstyle and color are to shine with glorious beauty so that you are captivating. The essence of a woman's captivating beauty reflects God's character and nature. Your hair is part of God's glory that reflects His character and nature that attracts people's attention. This week, ask Holy Spirit and others about your hair and how it can be at its best at this time in your life. If you have been doing a lot of complaining about your hair texture, color or quality, ask Holy Spirit to change your attitude. Every time you brush or comb your hair this week, remember Jesus is enthralled by your beauty.

Going Deeper: Psalm 45:11, Proverbs 20:29(CEV)[1], 1 Corinthians 11:15. What is God saying specifically to your heart as you read?

Prayer Time: Ask Holy Spirit for creative ideas on how to care for your hair so that it is the best it can be. Be sure and have fun!

---

1 Contemporary English Version

HANDS

"I arose to open for my lover, and my hands dripped with myrrh, my fingers with flowing myrrh, on the handles of the lock."

(Song of Solomon 5:5, NIV)

Open hands, loving hands, caring hands, comforting hands, giving hands, industrious hands, creative hands, healing hands bring all kinds of beauty through us and to us. The verse above speaks of these hands as being anointed with myrrh. Ask the Holy Spirit what specific beautiful anointing He has imparted to your hands. An anointing is a specific gift God has given to you to bring a revelation of His character and nature to this world. This week, pamper your hands with pleasing aromatic lotions. Use a different lotion for each anointing you know that you have received. Ask Holy Spirit if there is something that He wants to share with you about the anointing on your hands that you have not known. Ask a good friend what anointing she has seen in your hands. Tell others what you see in their anointed hands and encourage them. Be intentional about sharing the love and beauty of God through your hands as the Holy Spirit directs.

Going Deeper: Psalm 26:6-7, Psalm 78:72, Psalm 90:17. What is God revealing to you in these scriptures?

Prayer Time: Ask Holy Spirit for a specific act of love that you can accomplish with your hands this week for a specific person.

FEET

"How beautiful on the mountains are the feet of those who bring good news, who proclaim peace, who bring good tidings, who proclaim salvation, who say to Zion, "Your God reigns!"

(Isaiah 52:7, NIV)

First we stand in God's goodness; then we walk in it. The beauty of our feet is that they take us to places where we can share the goodness, peace and salvation that God has placed within us. We are royalty as God's princesses, so we walk with dignity and honor and give it away to others. The Hebrew word for the salvation that we are to proclaim, is Yeshua, which is the Hebrew name of Jesus. Yeshua/salvation means: protecting, rescue, aid, victory, prosperity, health and help.[1] This week pamper your feet with lotions, nail polish or new shoes. Be intentional about having your feet take you to share the beauty of good news, peace and

1 Strong, James, S.T.D., LL.D., Strongs Hebrew and Greek Dictionaries, e-Sword, Dictionary, "Yeshua", H3444

salvation that is within you. Stand in places of beauty on purpose!

Going Deeper: Psalm 17:5, Psalm 18:33, Song of Solomon 7:1. What is God saying specifically to your heart as you read?

Prayer Time: Ask Holy Spirit for specific places he would have you walk or stand. Then ask Him for creative ideas to bring good news, proclaim peace, bring good tidings or to proclaim salvation.

Heart

"Above all else, guard your heart, for it is the wellspring of life."* *(Proverbs 4:23, NIV)

Purpose to post a guard around your heart that only lets in that which will promote love and beauty. This guard must not be a guard of fear, anger or anxiety lest they rob you of the life you are promised. Rather, the precious jewel of your heart is to be guarded with integrity, honor, wisdom and love. Allow the Holy Spirit to check your heart guards within you. Discharge any guards that are not worthy and replace them with guards that increase your heart's brilliance! Wear heart jewelry this week as a reminder of just how precious your heart is to God and the treasure it is to you.

Going Deeper: Psalm 51:10, Proverbs 2:10, Matthew 5:8. What is Holy Spirit revealing to you through these scriptures?

Prayer Time: Ask Father God, Jesus and Holy Spirit, each one of the Trinity, how they see your heart. Then ask each one of the Trinity to show you how each protects your heart. Write down what you learn in a journal.

SKIN

"Your body is a chalice, wine-filled. Your skin is silken and tawny like a field of wheat touched by the breeze."

(Song of Solomon 7:2, The Message)

You have heard the saying that "beauty is only skin deep," but we have learned that beauty is multi-layered. The outward appearance needs lots of moisture, just the right amount of sun, and possibly some enhancing facial cosmetics to look its best. Finding out what brings out a beautiful appearance is a lifelong journey. We can learn what looks best from trial and error, friends and God. Our job is to maximize what God has given us, not for the sake of vanity, but rather for the glory of God. The same can be applied to our inner beauty. This week evaluate if your inner self is getting enough "Water of the Word"[1]and the "radiance of God's glory."[2] When the wind of the Spirit blows

1 Ephesians 5:26

2 Hebrews 1:3

upon your well-cared for soul, the effect will be stunning! Have a makeup party this week with friends, and enjoy the process of finding out from each other what brings out the most beauty.

Going Deeper: Isaiah 58:11, Isaiah 60:1. What is God saying specifically to your heart as you read?

Prayer Time: Give thanks to God for the beauty of skin. Sing praises to God with gratitude in your heart focusing on what God shared with you in this devotion.

Eyes

"You have stolen my heart, my sister, my bride; you have stolen my heart with one glance of your eyes..." (Song of Solomon4:9, NIV)

It has been said that "the eyes are the window of the soul." In the verse above, it takes just one glance to communicate love, purity, desire and delight, and the King's heart is swept away. We speak volumes with our eyes. What are we saying? Do we have the eyes of one who knows she is passionately loved? God loves you with an everlasting love that has great depth, width, length and breadth. As you put on eye makeup this week, look at your eyes in the mirror and notice the love that is reflected in them. How deep is that love? If you want more love, all you have to do is ask Holy Spirit to fill you up with the love of the Trinity so that even unconsciously, your eyes will speak the language of a woman in love.

Going Deeper: Matthew 6:22, Ephesians 1:17-23, Ephesians 3:16-21. What specific words of love is the Holy Spirit speaking to you as you read?

Prayer Time: Ask Holy Spirit to increase your awareness of His love for you. Then ask Him that His love in you will radiate from your eyes towards Him and others.

Jewelry

Earrings of Faith

"Your cheeks are beautiful with earrings, your neck with strings of jewels. We will make you earrings of gold, studded with silver."
(Song of Songs 1:10-11, NIV)

This passage seems to be in direct contrast to 1 Peter 3:3 where Peter is admonishing women not to wear jewelry. Actually, he is saying that our beauty should not depend on jewelry or fine clothes; rather, our beauty should come from within and shine outward. There is jewelry that draws attention to itself rather than the wearer. It actually detracts from the beauty of the wearer. God loves to adorn His children with precious stones to proclaim the beauty that reflects His glory. Earrings of gold studded with silver can remind us of the deep faith that is tried in fire and comes out pure gold.[1] These earrings can also

1 1 Peter 1:7 NIV

remind us of our ability to listen attentively to God and others. This week wear silver and gold earrings that reflect the beauty of faith to remind you that you have the ear of God listening for your words of love to Him and others.

Going Deeper: Proverbs 25:11-12, John 10:27 , 1 Peter 1:7. What is being revealed to you by the Holy Spirit in these scriptures?

Prayer Time: Speak words of love to God that He is longing to hear from you.

Necklace of Love

"You have stolen (ravished) my heart, my sister, my bride; you have stolen (ravished) my heart with one glance of your eyes, with one jewel of your necklace."

(Song of Songs 4:9, NIV)

A man in love will give the woman of his affections gifts to reflect his passion for her. Every time the gift is seen by him, he is reminded of his great love for her, which stirs up his passion for her anew. God is passionately in love with you! His heart is ravished with this love for you! When he sees the precious jewel of the life of His Son in you, it awakens the passion of His sacrificial love. Wear necklaces this week that symbolize God's love for you. Stir up your passion for Him by dwelling upon His passion for you.

Going Deeper: Luke 22:19-20, Romans 6:23, James 1:17. How is Jesus expressing His love for you in these scriptures?

Prayer Time: Ask Holy Spirit to reveal more of Jesus' passionate heart towards you. Write down what you hear.

JEWEL OF KNOWLEDGE

"Gold there is, and rubies in abundance, but lips that speak knowledge are a rare jewel." (Proverbs 20:15, NIV)

According to the Word Study Dictionary the word "knowledge" is described as: "knowing, learning, discernment, insight, and notion... God's gift of technical or specific knowledge along with wisdom and understanding..."[1] The most beautiful knowledge is mixed with humility and timeliness. Knowledge can be learned through study of a subject, life experiences or hands-on training. This week, ask Holy Spirit to show you the beautiful knowledge that you already possess and that is to be shared with others. Then ask which knowledge he wants you to acquire through study or practical application. Take steps of action to reach your goal and desire. Wear jewelry as a reminder of

1 The Word Study Dictionary. (Chattanooga, TN. AMG International Inc., Revised Edition 1993), e-Sword, Dictionary, "Da'at", H1847

the knowledge you have received and what new knowledge you are about to receive.

Going Deeper: Exodus 31:1-5, Proverbs 2:1-6, Philippians 1:9-11. What understanding is Holy Spirit giving you in these scriptures?

Prayer Time: Give thanks to God for the teaching and training you have received. Pray for specific knowledge that is a desire of your heart to acquire. Be sure and look for opportunities that God gives you to increase your understanding. Ask Holy Spirit what symbolic jewelry He would have you wear this week.

The Ruby of a Noble Character

"A wife of noble character who can find? She is worth far more than rubies." (Proverbs 31:10, NIV)

Although this verse is specific to those who have the title of "wife" anyone who has noble character is of great worth to God and others. The beauty of a ruby is formed with specific ingredients, temperature and pressure.[1] So it is with a noble character. To be noble, according to the Word Study Dictionary[2] and the Strong's Concordance,[3] means "to have valor, wealth, splendor, honor; to be virtuous, a force; to have strength and power". As we go through life, the combination of our

1 http://wiki.answers.com/Q/How_is_formed_in_nature (accessed February 25, 2013).

2 The Word Study Dictionary. (Chattanooga, TN. AMG International Inc., Revised Edition 1993), e-Sword, Dictionary, "Chayil", H2428

3 Strong, James, S.T.D., LL.D., Strongs Hebrew and Greek Dictionaries, e-Sword, Dictionary, "Chayil", H2428

unique environment, personality and the pressures we experience can create noble character. It all depends upon our choices. This week evaluate with the Holy Spirit if you have chosen to rise up to the nobility that He has offered. If not, then simply ask Holy Spirit to place His noble nature within you so that you will want to make noble choices from this day forward. Whenever you see a ruby, let it remind you of nobility purchased by Jesus for you to be absolutely beautiful.

Going Deeper: Ruth 3:11, Isaiah 32:8, Luke 8:15. What new revelation is God giving you in these scriptures?

Prayer Time: Meditate on the meaning of nobility and the art of being noble. Ask Holy Spirit if there are steps you need to take to walk more securely in the noble nature of King Jesus. Determine to take those steps with the help of the Holy Spirit.

CROWN OF BEAUTY

"to bestow on them a crown of beauty instead of ashes..."

(Isaiah 61:3, NIV)

In Old Testament Jewish culture people wore sackcloth and ashes in a time of despair.[1] The crown worn in this passage is a crown of victory over a time of great sorrow or mourning. This is a week to celebrate an area in your life where there was once great sorrow, but which God has turned into an area of great victory. Ask Holy Spirit to show you this area, and wear a crown this week in celebration. Be creative in your choice of a crown. It can be a garland, which people wore in victory. It can be a tiara of royalty. If you are going through a time of sorrow, wear the crown as a symbol of hope in the beauty yet to come into your life when Jesus has redeemed the time. When crowns are placed upon heads of royalty, there is typically a ceremony. You may want to create a ceremony with

1 Esther 4:1 NIV

friends with celebration and proclamations of the spiritual crowns God has given to you through His son Jesus Christ.

Going Deeper: Psalm 8:5, Psalm 103:4-5, Proverbs 4:7-9. What is God saying specifically to your heart as you read?

Prayer Time: Meditate on Jesus as your redeemer. Give thanks to God for His redeeming nature within you that places royal crowns upon your head.

Jewelry of Beauty

"I adorned you with jewelry: I put bracelets on your arms and a necklace around your neck..." (Ezekiel 16:11, NIV)

This passage is talking about God adorning the nation of Israel, but we can personalize it and realize that God has adorned us with beautiful things. Ask Holy Spirit what he has placed close to your heart that brings great beauty to your world. Ask Him what he has placed in your hands and arms that is beautiful. Celebrate these beautiful gifts by wearing bracelets and necklaces that symbolize the beauty within and without. Give away bracelets and necklaces in celebration!

Going Deeper: Psalm 18:30-35, Proverbs 3:3, Proverbs 31:17-20. What new understanding is God giving you in these scriptures?

Prayer Time: Ask Holy Spirit for creative ideas on how to celebrate God's beauty within you!

GIFTS OF LOVE FROM GOD

"...and I put a ring on your nose, earrings on your ears and a beautiful crown on your head..."

(Ezekiel 16:12, NIV)

Again this passage is speaking of the nation Israel, but again we will use this passage as God speaking to us personally. Each ornament mentioned in the scripture for today, represents God's love and adoration for you! He so loves to give you good gifts that represent the love relationship that He has with you or that He wants to have with you. Ask Holy Spirit to show you what new piece of jewelry He wants to give to you as a symbol of His great love for you. Then in anticipation for this new joy, by faith thank Him every day this week for this gift of love! You may see this jewelry in your mind's eye as a spiritual gift or it may be a physical gift with spiritual meaning. Position your heart and mind to receive this gift from God by faith. Regardless of how you receive it, rejoice and enjoy God's love for you! Be-loved!

Going Deeper: Song of Songs 5:9, Matthew 7:11, Romans 1:11. How is your faith strengthened by these scriptures?

Prayer Time: Ask God for greater faith and trust in His goodness towards you.

CLOTHING

GARMENT OF PRAISE

"...to bestow on them...a garment of praise instead of a spirit of despair."

(Isaiah 61:3, NIV)

The despair in this passage is one that is like a cloak of spiritual darkness, weakness and fearfulness. God wants you to exchange this spiritual rag of despair to a robe of glorious praise. Jesus' sacrifice on the cross and your acceptance of His salvation by faith allows Father God to joyfully place upon your shoulders the best robe of royalty (Luke 15:21). God does not want you to hang your head in despair, but rather to walk head held high, heart full of thanksgiving and praise. You are the beloved daughter of the King of the Universe! If you need to make the exchange of despair for praise, ask Holy Spirit to help you give to Jesus the spirit of despair, and put on the garment of praise. Rejoice in the beauty of praise on your shoulders instead of the weight of the world that Jesus bore for you.

Just for fun, imagine what your royal robe looks like. Draw a picture of it or describe it in words. You may want to go online and look at royal robes to get ideas.

Going Deeper: Matthew 27:28, Matthew 9:21, Luke 15:22. What is God saying specifically to your heart as you read?

Prayer Time: Praise God for the new royal wardrobe He has provided for you through His son Jesus.

Wedding Clothes

***"I delight greatly in the LORD;
my soul rejoices in my God.
For he has clothed me with garments of
salvation and arrayed me in a robe of righteousness,
as a bridegroom adorns his head like a priest,
and as a bride adorns herself with her jewels."***

(Isaiah 61:10, NIV)

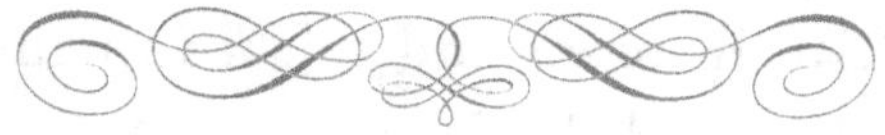

There is great joy in getting dressed up for your wedding! You want to look and feel your best in the clothes that you wear for this momentous occasion. It is the desire of every bride to dazzle her bridegroom with how she looks, so that when he looks at her it takes his breath away! God has clothed us with salvation and righteousness so that we dazzle the universe with the beauty of His relationship with us. These glorious clothes fit perfectly. Just wearing them brings deep comfort and great joy to your soul, because you are who you were created to be. This week, wear clothes that make you look and feel good. Rejoice in the realization that the Church is the bride of Christ.

If you are in relationship with Jesus, then the Holy Spirit is dressing you for Jesus' return for His bride! You are being fitted for your wedding gown of heaven and you are breathtakingly beautiful (full of beauty).

Going Deeper: Psalm 45, Ephesians 5:25-27, Revelation 19:7-9. How is God revealing His love for you in these scriptures?

Prayer Time: Ask Holy Spirit to help you pick out your clothes to wear this week. Listen for Him to tell you the specific reasons he has for His clothing choices. Write it down and rejoice in the intimacy between you and Holy Spirit.

Designer Clothing

"So, chosen by God for this new life of love, dress in the wardrobe God picked out for you: compassion, kindness, humility, quiet strength, discipline."

(Colossians 3:12, The Message)

To be chosen by God implies that you are His favorite! He wants you to try on the new clothes that Jesus paid for! The Holy Spirit is holding out these bright new clothes for you to try on and get comfortable in. The compassion ensemble that you sink into is God's deep, heart-felt love for people. Kindness is the designer's dream for everyone to be wearing. Humility is beautiful on anyone. Yes, one size fits all! Quiet strength is another way of saying gentleness. This life has enough harshness that when gentleness is worn, it is noticeably appreciated. Put your running clothes on with discipline/patience/long suffering/forbearance. Go the distance with yourself and others so that the beauty within has the necessary time to acquire fullness of joy. This week choose colors of clothing to represent each godly characteristic. Be conscious of your clothes representing the royalty of heaven.

Going Deeper: Psalm 145:9, Titus 3:4-8, Hebrews 12:1. Ask Holy Spirit to highlight one particular character trait in the devotion of today that he wants to bring to your attention. Then ask Him to show you a new and fresh way to wear this ensemble of grace.

Prayer Time: Ask Holy Spirit for divine appointments to give away the godly characteristics mentioned in this devotion. Write down these God encounters in a journal.

Details of Beauty

"I clothed you with an embroidered dress and put leather sandals on you. I dressed you in fine linen and covered you with costly garments."

(Ezekiel 16:10, NIV)

God desires to clothe you in the best possible spiritual clothes. Embroidery represents intricacy and detailed beauty. The costly garments may represent silk, which comes from an incredible costly creative process. God goes to great lengths to clothe you in beauty. He delights in the unique details. This week, wear any or all of the above: embroidered clothing, beautiful shoes or special clothes. When you do, remember God delights in the details of creating beauty in you, upon you and around you. Ask Holy Spirit to point out details of beauty in your life that you have not noticed before. Share your discoveries with a friend.

Going Deeper: 1 Chronicles 28:19, Proverbs 31:22, Ephesians 6:15. What specific detail is God highlighting for you in these scriptures?

Prayer Time: Give thanks to God for the beautiful details in your life.

PROVISION

"And why do you worry about clothes? See how the lilies of the field grow. They do not labor or spin. Yet I tell you that not even Solomon in all his splendor was dressed like one of these. If that is how God clothes the grass of the field, which is here today and tomorrow is thrown into the fire, will he not much more clothe you,
O you of little faith? So do not worry, saying, ' What shall we eat?' or 'What shall we drink?' or 'What shall we wear?' For the pagans run after all these things, and your heavenly Father knows that you need them. But seek first his kingdom and his righteousness, and all these things will be given to you as well."

(Matthew 6:28-33, NIV)

Fashion, Fashion, Fashion! Chasing after what is new, bigger, better. Shopping and buying to make us feel better. Those of us in first nations probably have enough shoes and clothes in our closets to supply a third world village. This is not to be read with the filter of guilt. Rather, we need to be reminded of how blessed we are and share the wealth so that others can experience the beauty of God's provision through our lives. This week do some research and find people in need of clothes or shoes. Give them the best quality that their culture will allow. In doing this act of kindness, generosity and love, you will be seeking God's kingdom and righteousness. Notice how God gives us good feelings when we give away His goodness, goodness with which He's blessed us. This is the beauty of God's kingdom in you! If you are in need of clothes, worry will rob you of a blessing of God providing for you. Instead of worrying, trust God to bless you in unexpected ways this week; give thanks, by faith, for his loving care for you!

Going Deeper: Proverbs 11:25, Proverbs 19:17, 1 Timothy 6:17-19. Ask Holy Spirit to show you His joy in these scriptures.

Prayer Time: Ask Holy Spirit for specific people that you can give clothing to. Ask Him for a greater confidence in His provision for you and others.

ROYAL CLOTHING

"All glorious is the princess within her chamber; her gown is interwoven with gold."

(Psalm 45:13, NIV)

You are the daughter of the King! In the place of intimacy (chamber), God weaves together a beautiful gown with the gold of heaven! Setting aside time to be alone with God in a precious place of intimacy gives Him the opportunity to create within you golden opportunities of worship, wisdom, witty ideas, blessings, healings and many more treasures of His glory! This week set aside a time of intimacy with Father God, Jesus and Holy Spirit. Converse with God, sit at His feet and listen to His whispers of love. Worship Him and soak in His tender mercies. When you come out of your "chamber," you will wear the glorious, golden beauty of time spent with your Creator! Revel in this royal gown of glory! Wear clothing that has gold color in it or wear gold jewelry this week as a reminder of your intimacy with God.

Going Deeper: Job 37:22, Psalm 24, Revelation 1:12-16. The glory of God means all of His character and nature. "The glory of God is what He is essentially..."[1] What is God revealing to you in these scriptures?

Prayer Time: Create an intimate time with God. Worship and enjoy the King of glory!

1 The Word Study Dictionary. (Chattanooga, TN. AMG International Inc., Revised Edition 1993), e-Sword, Dictionary, "Doxa", G1391.

KINGDOM CLOTHING

"...her clothing is silk and purple."
(Proverbs 31:22, KJV)

Silk is smooth and purple is the color of royalty. This week give thanks to King Jesus because He has smoothed out difficulties in your life and raised you up to a place of honor. If you need Jesus to do this in your life, have others that you trust pray for you to be raised up and your circumstances to be aligned with the desires and blessings of your King. Wear silk or purple this week in celebration of your status in God's kingdom.

Going Deeper: Isaiah 40:4, Isaiah 42:16, Ephesians 2:6. Ask Holy Spirit to give you specific life applications for you with these scriptures.

Prayer Time: Ask Holy Spirit to reveal to you your status in the Kingdom of God. Then ask Him to help you rise up to all that He desires you to be.

Proverbs 31

Virtuous Woman

Trustworthy

"A wife of noble character who can find? She is worth far more than rubies. Her husband has full confidence in her and lacks nothing of value. She brings him good, not harm, all the days of her life."

(Proverbs 31:10-12, NIV)

Let us look at the larger context for this verse. It can definitely mean the relationship between a wife and husband, but it can also mean the relationship between a woman and her master. In modern life, it would indicate the relationship of a woman and her employer. So I would like to propose that this woman gives the man in her life no grief. His heart is secure in her bringing him well-being. A sense of confidence means that he has no worries about what she says or does because he knows that whatever she does or says will be for his good. The phrase, "lacks nothing of value," implies that she has fought to give him every good thing he has. To have a trustworthy character and nature are two of the most beautiful qualities a woman can have. People feel safe, secure and protected around her.

This week ask Holy Spirit for Jesus' character and nature of being trustworthy. Find a friend to keep you accountable and to pray for you in this area. If you sense from the Lord that you are already trustworthy, celebrate His goodness in you and upon you! You may want to get a stone that looks like a ruby or is a ruby, to remind you and to encourage you that you are trustworthy in Christ Jesus!

Going Deeper: Nehemiah 13:13, Proverbs 11 & 25:13, Luke 16:11-12 & 19:17. What is Holy Spirit revealing to you in these scriptures?

Prayer Time: Ask God for the royal family trait of trustworthiness. Then ask Holy Spirit to confirm in you that this character quality is yours forever through Christ Jesus.

____

____

____

____

WISE AND FAITHFUL

"She speaks with wisdom, and faithful instruction is on her tongue."

(Proverbs 31:26, NIV)

The beauty of speaking words of wisdom and faithful instruction come from a heart that seeks wisdom and faithful instruction. Great value must be placed in these qualities. We will speak out whatever is important to us. What is on the tip of your tongue? What have you often been dwelling on or thinking about? Is your mind beautiful? Do you like to spend time with yourself? Isn't it amazing that we have a relationship with ourselves as well as with others? This week, determine to make your mind a beautiful place in which to be. Fill your mind with beautiful thoughts, music, movies, words and actions. As you dwell on beauty in your mind, beautiful words and faithful instruction will be on the tip of your tongue. There will be a natural flow from whatever source you drink. Ask Holy Spirit to help you drink frequently from His "river of delights"[1] in order to delight yourself as well as others. Wisdom is free for the asking, so ask for wisdom often.[2]

Going Deeper: Proverbs 4:13, John 4, John 7:37-39. How is Jesus speaking words of love to you in these scriptures?

Prayer Time: Ask Holy Spirit to show you what specifically He wants you to fill your mind with.

1 Psalm 36:8 NIV

2 James 1:5 NIV

Industrious

"She selects wool and flax and works with eager hands. She is like the merchant ships, bringing her food from afar. She gets up while it is still dark; she provides food for her family and portions for her servant girls. She considers a field and buys it; out of her earnings she plants a vineyard. She sets about her work vigorously; her arms are strong for her tasks. She sees that her trading is profitable, and her lamp does not go out at night. In her hand she holds the distaff and grasps the spindle with her fingers."

(Proverbs 31:13-19, NIV)

Wow, this is a busy woman! When I look at this woman, I joke with my friends that if I had servant girls I could be a lot more productive! But this is a woman with purpose, and she enjoys her work and the sense of accomplishment it brings her. God has built within each one of us the beauty of completing a task and knowing it is a job well done. If the job is not well done, there is not a fullness of joy for us or others. Each one of us is good at something, whether it is being a mother, worker, employer or the best "you" you can be. This week, explore areas where you could be giving your best. Sometimes that means you need to take a break from your toil and get some rest so you can do your best. Sometimes it means brainstorming for new ideas and new avenues. Sometimes it means healing from hurts so you can give your best to others. Whatever it is, take steps this week to be the best you can be. The world is poorer without the beauty only you can bring! You are important and beautiful!

Going Deeper: Deuteronomy 16:15, Ruth 2, Titus 2:3-5 (MSG) What are you learning in these scriptures?

Prayer Time: Ask Holy Spirit to give you a joyful plan to bring out more beauty in your life. Write it down and refer to it often.

____

____

____

____

____

____

Generous

"She opens her arms to the poor and extends her hands to the needy."
(Proverbs 31:20, NIV)

Have you ever felt the tug of helping out someone less fortunate than yourself? That emotion is God-given compassion. There is a beautiful art in giving to the needy that takes discernment as well as compassion. The beauty of it not only relies on the good feeling that we receive that God has built within us when we give, but also on the satisfaction of knowing that the helping hand you give is doing the recipient the most good. We may have baggage in the area of giving to others, such as cynicism, which can creep in when you have given to someone in need and the recipient took advantage of your kindness. Clear your heart of any negative emotion in this area by laying all trespasses at Jesus' feet. Jesus' secret of self-sacrifice was to scorn the shame for the joy set before Him (Hebrews 12:2). There must be a liberal offering of honor and dignity to all when giving to the poor. We need to maximize God's glorious beauty by portraying His generous and discerning nature. This week, listen to the Holy Spirit and He will show you where He wants you to open your arms and where He wants you to extend your hand to the needy. Then take action with confidence!

Going Deeper: Proverbs 19:17, Proverbs 22:9, Matthew 25:31-40. Where is Holy Spirit touching your heart with His compassion as you read these scriptures?

Prayer Time: Ask Holy Spirit for specific instructions. Write down whom He wants you to give to and what He wants you to give to them. Then ask Him to help you to follow through. You may want to do this with others to increase the joy in giving.

Prepared

"When it snows, she has no fear for her household; for all of them are clothed in scarlet. She makes coverings for her bed; she is clothed in fine linen and purple."

(Proverbs 31:21-22, NIV)

The beauty of being prepared is to think ahead and to plan. This woman thought ahead to when "the snow was going to fall" and imagined her family in beautiful winter clothes and bed coverings that were warm and comfortable. A woman's home decor sets the atmosphere for her family and others. Just as God has created a beautiful atmosphere for us with sunsets, sunrises, moonlight, forests and the sea so a woman plans the beauty in her home to bless everyone. This week, dream about the future for your family and what they will be wearing and what will surround them. If you are talented in this area then God has graced your hands and heart with this beauty. If you are not adept in this skill, then find someone you trust who is and have her help you create the atmosphere that you want in your home. If you lack the funds to buy things, ask Holy Spirit to help you with creativity with what you have around you. Dream, plan, prepare, implement and enjoy the beauty of your home.

Going Deeper: Psalm 128, Proverbs 14:1, Proverbs 24:3-4. What is God saying specifically to your heart as you read?

Prayer Time: Ask Holy Spirit to give you creative ideas of home décor.

Strength and Dignity

"She is clothed with strength and dignity; she can laugh at the days to come." (Proverbs 31:25, NIV)

Strength=internal fortitude[1]

Dignity=magnificence[2]

These are part of the Hebrew definitions of strength and dignity in this passage. To develop internal fortitude implies that every event in our lives resurrects an internal structure within us. If this structure is solid in God's truth and grace, it will stand in the trials of life, and joyous laughter will ring in its walls. You were created for magnificence and dignity, which means when your character is magnified it shines with the glory that God was

1 The Word Study Dictionary. (Chattanooga, TN. AMG International Inc., Revised Edition 1993), e-Sword, Dictionary, "Oz", H5797.

2 Strong, James, S.T.D., LL.D., Strongs Hebrew and Greek Dictionaries, e-Sword, Dictionary, "Hadar", H1926.

thinking of when he created you. Our daily choices will include attitudes, values and faith. These will determine the strength and dignity with which we are clothed. What kind of spiritual clothing do you wear daily? See if you need to change your spiritual clothing with the help of the Holy Spirit. Give Jesus your rags of unforgiveness, bitterness, anxiety and fear, all of which make you weak and dull. Put on the royal robes of righteousness, and shine! This week, wear clothing that symbolizes strength and dignity. Laugh often and loud with JOY at the days to come! Be purposeful in your heart to give away strength and dignity to others.

Going Deeper: Nehemiah 8:10, Psalm 28:7, Proverbs 17:22. What is God saying specifically to your heart in these scriptures?

Prayer Time: Have someone you trust pray for you this week in the area of strength and dignity.

Honored and Honoring

"Her children arise and call her blessed; her husband also, and he praises her: Many women do noble things, but you surpass them all. Charm is deceptive, and beauty is fleeting; but a woman who fears the LORD is to be praised. Give her the reward she has earned, and let her works bring her praise at the city gate." (Proverbs 31:28-31 NIV)

Another word for blessed is happy.[1] Do children know you as a happy person? Does praise come your way from men, be it your husband or others? Do you consider what you do as noble? Do you fear the Lord? Evaluate your beauty of character at home, in the workplace and in your community. If you fall short in areas, do not be surprised. Your human nature needs a redemptive Savior to bring out the glorious beauty that He designed in you

1 Strong, James, S.T.D., LL.D., Strongs Hebrew and Greek Dictionaries, e-Sword, Dictionary, "Asher", H833.

and for you. In order to be honored at the end of our lives, we must live an honorable life. Picture yourself at the end of your life looking back with the satisfaction of knowing you lived an honorable life. What choices do you need to make today in order to fulfill this vision? Ask your Savior, Jesus, to make the necessary changes in your heart and life to be the woman of honor He sees in you. Rise up, woman of God, and be all that you can be!

Going Deeper: Psalm 8:5, Psalm 62:7, Matthew 5:3-10. What is God revealing to you in these scriptures?

Prayer Time: Ask Holy Spirit to help you make any changes necessary to live a life of honor. Honor the Lord in prayer and praises.

Queen Esther

Form & Features

"...This girl, who was also known as Esther, was lovely in form and features..."

(Esther 2:7)

Each one of us is given a unique form and features. Many of us spend way too much time bemoaning what we don't have. This focus can waste time, thought and energy. Instead of focusing on what we think is wrong with us, let us focus on how to maximize the form and features God has given us. Write down what you think are your best features; then ask someone who loves you to tell you what he or she appreciates about you.

The secret of defeating negativity about our bodies is inspiration. Let's break down that word: in-spire. We see spires of churches to encourage people to look up to God. To be truly inspired we need to have an inner compass that lifts up our heads instead of looking down on ourselves or others. There are several ways to be inspired, and here are a few:

1. Choose a favorite Bible verse between you and the Holy Spirit to encourage yourself to look up and be encouraged (full of courage). Ask Him to bring it to mind when needed.

2. Be intentional about choosing friends who will encourage and inspire you to be your best.

3. Read about or watch others who are inspiring in the area in which you need encouragement.

This week make intentional choices to be inspired and inspiring.

Going Deeper: Psalm 3:3, 1 Thessalonians 1:3, 2 Thessalonians 2:16-17. What inspiration or encouragement do you receive in these scriptures?

Prayer Time: Ask Holy Spirit for inspiration for a specific area of beauty in your life. Give thanks to God for specific inspiration in your life that you have already received and by faith what you will receive.

___

___

___

Favor

"The girl pleased him and won his favor…And Esther won the favor of everyone who saw her."
(Esther 5:2, NIV)

"And it was so, when the king saw Esther the queen standing in the court, that she obtained favor in his sight; and the king held out to Esther the golden sceptre that was in his hand. So Esther drew near, and touched the top of the sceptre"
(Esther 2:9a & 15b, KJV)

The Hebrew meaning of favor is: grace, kindness, precious and beauty.[1] Favor and grace come from Father God. As the saying goes "beauty is in the eye of the beholder," and God finds you absolutely stunning! He gives you grace and favor before and

1 Strong, James, S.T.D., LL.D., Strongs Hebrew and Greek Dictionaries, e-Sword, Dictionary, "Chen", H2580.

after you step into His presence. He gives you His scepter of authority through His son, Jesus, and you, in turn, extend the grace and beauty of His kingdom to those around you. This week, seek God's presence. Be particularly mindful of the beautiful favor you receive from The King. Present your requests to Him with the joy of knowing He loves you deeply. Pray for favor in the areas of your life where you know you need it. Then ask Holy Spirit to reveal to you where He wants to give you favor that you have not previously thought of. Write it down or share with a friend. Expect and look for favor and be thankful when it comes!

Going Deeper: Psalm 5:12, Luke 2:14, 2 Corinthians 6:2. What is Holy Spirit revealing to you in these scriptures?

Prayer Time: Ask for God's favor in specific areas of your life. Then look for the answer to this prayer with expectation and joy.

Influence

"The girl pleased him and won his favor. Immediately he provided her with her beauty treatments and special food. He assigned to her seven maids selected from the king's palace and moved her and her maids into the best place in the harem."

(Esther 2:15, NIV)

"When the turn came for Esther... to go to the king, she asked for nothing other than what Hegai, the king's eunuch who was in charge of the harem, suggested. And Esther won the favor of everyone who saw her."

(Esther 2:9, NIV)

The definition of influence is to have a compelling force or power over people or things.[1] In the story of Esther, Hegai had direct influence over her beauty treatments so that she would please the king. Esther valued what Hegai suggested and took his counsel and advice. Esther was also surrounded by maids who were handpicked by Hegai. These girls would have influence upon Esther's beauty process as well. It is important whom we surround ourselves with and from whom we take counsel. There are particular people whom God will place in our lives who will bring out the best in us so that we shine with the beauty that God meant for us to have. This week, evaluate who has the most influence in your life. Do they bring out the best in you? Why or why not? Do you bring out the best in them? Why or why not? Choose to be influenced by people who bring out the best in you. This week consider who your mentors are or who you would want to mentor you in specific areas to bring out the very best in your inner and outer beauty. You may want to connect with a mentor this week to continue your journey of beauty in this world.

Going Deeper: Psalm 32:8, Proverbs 27:9, Titus 2. What is God saying to you in these scriptures?

---

1 http://dictionary.reference.com/browse/influence (accessed February 25, 2013).

Prayer Time: Give thanks to God for mentors that bring out the beauty of Christ Jesus in you. Ask Him to help you bring out more beauty in others.

Position

"For if you remain silent at this time, relief and deliverance for the Jews will arise from another place, but you and your father's family will perish. And who knows but that you have come to royal position for such a time as this?"

(Esther 4:14)

Where has God positioned you in your home, work, ministry and community? Are you aware of the beauty, salvation and honor that He wants you to share in these spheres? You were created at this time in this environment for a purpose of great consequence. This week, find out from Holy Spirit where He has positioned you at this time in history to bring influence and the beauty of heaven to earth. Discuss this with a close friend or friends and plan how to maximize your assignments from God. Encourage each other and pray for one another and celebrate your uniquely beautiful positions!

Going Deeper: I Chronicles 12:32, John 17:4, Ephesians 2:10. What is the Holy Spirit teaching you in these scriptures?

Prayer Time: Ask for a deeper awareness of the influence you have to bring out beauty in others. Ask God for His grace to carry out your assignment on earth with beauty and grace.

HONOR AND BRAVERY

"Then Esther sent this reply to Mordecai: 'Go, gather together all the Jews who are in Susa, and fast for me. Do not eat or drink for three days, night or day. I and my maids will fast as you do. When this is done, I will go to the king, even though it is against the law. And if I perish, I perish.'"

(Esther 4:15-16)

Sometimes we are called upon to make sacrifices for the benefit of others, be they large or small. The beauty of sacrifice is in the purity of heart (honor) and nobleness of purpose (bravery). It takes wisdom and prayer to determine both. Wisdom is free for the asking (James 1:5), but prayer is costly. It is good to remember that the beauty of God's wisdom lines up with His character and nature. Prayer takes time and focus so it is good to plan to pray. This week, think of someone in your life who showed you honor and was brave in doing so. Let them know how much you appreciate their courage and care. Ask Holy Spirit to make you a woman of honor and bravery. If a specific area is brought to your mind where you need to be brave and honorable, ask for wisdom and listen for instructions. Write down steps you need to take and follow through by acting upon them.

Going Deeper: John 15:12-13, Romans 5:8, James 3:17-18. What is God saying to you in these scriptures?

Prayer Time: Ask Holy Spirit if there is a sacrifice of love and time he would have you make on behalf of another.

Timing

Esther replied, "My petition and my request is this: If the king regards me with favor and if it pleases the king to grant my petition and fulfill my request, let the king and Haman come tomorrow to the banquet I will prepare for them. Then I will answer the king's question."

(Esther 5:7-8)

There is beauty in right timing. Queen Esther waited for the right moment to present her request to the king. Speaking or acting too soon or too late will not bring about a good result or fullness of joy. We all know that if people are late in remembering our birthdays it sometimes does not bring the fullness of joy as remembering our birthdays on the proper day. When we do not wait for the proper day for intimacy between a man and a woman there is joy stolen. God has built into each one of us a maximum of beauty in waiting for the right moment to speak or to act. One of the ways to cultivate this beauty is to make right timing a personal value. This week, be aware of people saying the right thing at the right time. If appropriate, compliment them for this quality. Notice when you do the right thing for the right reasons at the right time. Revel in the fullness of joy it brings and know that your Creator built this beauty into you!

Going Deeper: Ecclesiastes 8:5-6, Habakkuk 2:3 John 7:2-8. What is Holy Spirit revealing to you about timing in these scriptures?

Prayer Time: Thank God for His perfect timing for fullness of joy. Ask Holy Spirit for the ability to wait upon The Lord to renew your strength (Isaiah 40:31) when waiting for the right time.

LEGACY

"Esther's decree confirmed these regulations about Purim, and it was written down in the records."

(Esther 9:32)

The feast of Purim is still celebrated today by Jews. Esther left a legacy to Christians and Jews with her life choices. She may not have realized it at the time how she would impact the world, but her selfless act saved a nation and has been preserved as Holy Scripture. We, too, can leave a legacy of beauty behind us through our choices of today. This week, consider what you would like to leave behind on this earth when your shift is over. Write out a backwards strategy- this is where you write the goal first and then the steps to reach the goal. Put these steps in order 1 through 10, or as many steps as you think you need to attain the goal. Make plans to carry out the first step. Give yourself a deadline and make yourself accountable to someone. When you finish each step, celebrate and enjoy the journey!

Going Deeper: Proverbs 13:22, Isaiah 61:7, Mark 14:9. What insight and understanding is Holy Spirit imparting to you in these scriptures?

Prayer Time: Ask God what He wants you to leave behind as a legacy to others.

Congratulations for completing spiritual and physical beauty treatments! What devotion was the most impactful? What truth was the most enlightening? What physical beauty treatment had special meaning to you? How have you been transformed into royal beauty? Share the answers to these questions with others or write them in your journal.

After Queen Esther went through her beauty treatments, she was presented to the King. He was attracted to her and she won his favor and approval. He placed a crown upon her head and proclaimed her queen. He gave a great banquet for all of his nobles and officials and called it Esther's banquet. He proclaimed a royal holiday throughout the land and distributed gifts with "royal liberality."[1]

Now it is time to celebrate your transformation into royal beauty! Create a memorable event using Queen Esther's story as a springboard. Be sure and ask Holy Spirit to give you creative ideas. He loves to partner with you in planning a celebration.

Step into your position of "Queen" in the Kingdom of God. Continue to walk into new vistas of beauty throughout your life and you will leave a royal legacy of beauty in heaven and on earth.

---

1 Esther 2:17, 18 NIV

REFERENCES

1769 King James Version of The Holy Bible, e-Sword, Bible, http://www.e-sword.net/

Essential Oils Desk Reference, (Essential Science Publishing, 2006)

Johann (C.F.) Keil and Franz Delitzsch, Keil & Delitzsch Commentary on the Old Testament, e-Sword, Commentary, http://www.e-sword.net/

Strong, James, S.T.D., LL.D., Strongs Hebrew and Greek Dictionaries, e-Sword, Dictionary, http://www.e-sword.net/

The Contemporary English Version, e-Sword, Bible, http://www.e-sword.net/

The Holy Bible, New International Version, e-Sword, Bible, http://www.e-sword.net/

The Message: The Bible in Contemporary Language, e-Sword, Bible, http://www.e-sword.net/

The Word Study Dictionary. (Chattanooga, TN. AMG International Inc., Revised Edition 1993), e-Sword, Dictionary, http://www.e-sword.net/

RECOMMENDED

READING

Captivating: Unveiling the Mystery of the Woman's Soul by John & Stasi Eldredge

About the Author

Dixie Nash has a heart for God, His Word, and people. Her joy is to watch others grow in their knowledge of God's love for them as uniquely created individuals. Her background as a professional counselor has given her insights into people's needs both emotionally and spiritually. She especially likes to bring the Joy of the Lord into her speaking to lift others up.

Dixie and her husband, Jim, planted a Nazarene church, where Dixie was the pastor for seven years. The next adventure for this couple led them to Discipleship Training School with Youth With A Mission (YWAM). Their outreach took them to England, Uganda and Spain. Dixie furthered her training in YWAM by completing the School of Evangelism. Her outreach with this school was in England during the 2012 summer Olympics.

God has placed a great compassion in Dixie and Jim for the Shepherds of God's flock. They have an International ministry called Shepherd Watch that encourages and supports pastors and missionaries. They currently serve shepherds in two countries, India and Nepal.

If you would like to share a testimony or book Dixie for a speaking engagement please visit her website at www.spiritualbeautytreatments.com.